Advanced Exercises in Practical English Grammar 1

A. J. Thomson and A. V. Martinet

Advanced Exercises in Practical English Grammar 1

New Edition

Cornelsen &
Oxford University Press

Alleinberechtigte Ausgabe für die Bundesrepublik Deutschland und Österreich.

(Die Originalausgabe wurde veröffentlicht im Verlag Oxford University Press, Oxford.)

Zu Practical English Grammar – School Edition – gehören:

A Practical English Grammar – School Edition –
Best.-Nr. 23214

Advanced Exercises in Practical English Grammar 1
Best.-Nr. 23222

Advanced Exercises in Practical English Grammar 2
Best.-Nr. 23230

Die Advanced Exercises 1 und 2 sind ebenfalls verwendbar in Verbindung mit der umfangreicheren Originalausgabe von A Practical English Grammar (Third Edition), die unter der Bestellnummer 22340 lieferbar ist.

2. Auflage 1983
Bestellnummer 23222

Filmset by Tradespools Ltd, Frome, Somerset, England
and printed in Hong Kong

ISBN 3–8109–2322–2

Vertrieb für die Bundesrepublik Deutschland einschließlich Berlin (West), Österreich und die Schweiz:
Cornelsen-Velhagen & Klasing Verlagsgesellschaft, Bielefeld

A. J. Thomson and A. V. Martinet

Advanced Exercises in Practical English Grammar 1

New Edition

Key

Cornelsen &
Oxford University Press

Key

1 Present and past tenses

Exercise 7 1 don't build, use 2 is having 3 drinks, is drinking 4 does she do, plays, watches 5 is raining, haven't 6 leaves 7 speaks, don't understand 8 is making, makes 9 wears 10 don't like 11 am wearing 12 is reading 13 am papering 14 is boiling 15 are you enjoying, am enjoying, want 16 do you get, go, am going 17 are you putting, am going, are you coming, do you mind 18 do you owe, I owe, do you intend 19 do you belong, do you read, do you change, I change 20 learns, doesn't seem 21 always buy/am always buying, win 22 do you like, am giving 23 promise, promise 24 do you always write 25 do you love, like, don't love 26 do you dream, dream, eat, have 27 is whistling, is feeling 28 are always complaining/always complain 29 are using 30 is always saying/always says, does 31 do you know, falls 32 are you writing, write, do you want 33 are having, wonder, are talking 34 do you believe, don't believe, do you read 35 is making, do you think, doesn't matter, makes 36 is smoking, expect, are building, are always doing/always do, don't you put, remove

Exercise 8 1 does Tom think, thinks, agree 2 does this one cost, it costs 3 do you hear, is blowing 4 do you see, am looking, don't see 5 listens, is always thinking 6 deserts, goes 7 do you understand, don't understand 8 do you have, eat, drink 9 rises, see, are picketing 10 are you walking, walk, am hurrying, am meeting, doesn't like 11 wish, keeps, think, wants 12 do you recognize, think, don't remember 13 isn't coming, gets 14 is waiting, want 15 don't you see, see, am not wearing, does it say, says 16 is always borrowing/always borrows, remembers 17 do you need, do you feel 18 does it save, take, doesn't matter 19 am saving, am going 20 think, are getting 21 are looking, is just taking 22 does, is always working 23 is he doing, think, is polishing 24 is coming, do you want 25 is Peter getting on, seems 26 is Mrs Pitt looking/does Mrs Pitt look, is smoking, (is) dropping 27 leave, arrive, spend, set, sounds, get 28 makes, finds, goes, does not forget, returns, looks 29 finds, recognizes, coils, kills 30 does the snake feel, don't know, ends 31 do you end, begins, put, prefers 32 does the word 'catastrophe' mean, means 33 are you waiting, am waiting, doesn't open, know, want, starts/is starting 34 are you smoking, don't smoke, am smoking, want, removes 35 owns, don't know, uses, knows, owns 36 do you mind, ask, depends, concerns, refuse

Exercise 12 1 was burning 2 was writing 3 was making 4 left 5 was just leaving 6 was having, got, went 7 stood 8 was playing, insisted 9 was walking 10 was having, lunched 11 wore, carried 12 did you think, liked 13 shared, was always complaining/always complained 14 realized, was travelling 15 was playing, threw 16 was just opening, blew 17 was opening, heard, put, crawled 18 was looking, found 19 were you doing 20 were playing, heard, hid, took 21 was cleaning, went, killed 22 didn't allow, was blowing 23 was crossing/crossed, stepped, fell 24 was still lying, saw 25 saw, stopped 26 did you damage, ran, were driving, were going 27 was getting/got, started, fell 28 called, was already getting up 29 was mending/mended, got 30 heard, went, opened, didn't recognize, wasn't wearing 31 were sitting, was doing, was knitting, were reading, smiled, said 32 were dancing, broke, stole 33 knew, were looking, hid, went 34 was always buying 35 told, was spending/spent, listened 36 saw, was planting, was

Exercise 13 1 woke, was always getting/always got, went, bought 2 had to, usually grazed/was usually grazing 3 didn't normally chase, made, was crossing, went 4 annoyed, began 5 was carrying, was raining, threw, ran 6 stopped, began, was doing 7 awoke, was sitting, was looking, called, turned, smiled 8 did you interrupt, was having 9 was carrying, heard 10 was looking, noticed 11 were walking/walked, heard, turned, held, stopped 12 arrived, was waiting, was wearing, (was) looking/looked, saw, waved, shouted, was saying/said, was making 13 escaped, was working, was wearing 14 was travelling, began 15 didn't like, was trying 16 was making, felt, brought, was able 17 saw, was painting, did you like, was only just starting, saw 18 took, was being, were still listening, left/were leaving 19 was, had to, was enjoying 20 were coming, stopped, said, was looking, asked 21 saw, were you using, was using, were you riding 22 was knitting 23 was, said, hoped, was enjoying 24 was watering, began, put, went 25 was just writing, remembered, had 26 found, was digging, belonged 27 saw, was hurrying, asked, was going, said, was speaking, wasn't 28 called, was still working 29 came, was smoking, had, threw, hoped 30 noticed, was rising, were you smoking, came, asked 31 was swimming, stole, had to 32 said, were working, wanted 33 said, was building, thought 34 woke, said, thought, was trying 35 did you lend, was still reading, didn't know, were still reading 36 came, woke, started, woke, came, said, said, didn't hear, was barking, went, telephoned

Exercise 15 1 have, wound 2 haven't, ate 3 has, fed 4 haven't, have only repaired 5 have done, did 6 haven't, haven't found 7 have, made 8 haven't, have been 9 haven't, haven't seen 10 have, went 11 have driven, drove 12 hasn't, has, went 13 have, was 14 has, spoke 15 have only spent, have 16 haven't saved, have saved 17 hasn't, went 18 haven't seen, saw, didn't see 19 have, paid 20 haven't, flew 21 bit, has bitten 22 planted, haven't 23 has, wrote 24 haven't, drank, killed

Exercise 16 1 have you lived/have you been living, have lived/have been living 2 lived, went 3 did you wear, insisted 4 left, cut, have worn 5 wrote 6 has written, has just finished 7 flew, did you see 8 haven't seen 9 hasn't smoked 10 composed 11 did he arrive, arrived 12 did you lock 13 read, enjoyed 14 haven't finished 15 have never drunk 16 have written 17 has stopped 18 have just cleaned 19 left, got 20 did, was 21 has just gone 22 went 23 have you had, had 24 met 25 did you see 26 began, lasted, enjoyed 27 has just begun 28 has the newspaper come 29 arrived, started 30 has been 31 wrote 32 have missed 33 broke 34 has been 35 worked, retired, went 36 have you been, spent, did you have, stopped

Exercise 17 1 haven't seen, told 2 bought, did you pay, paid 3 did you find, found, didn't you leave 4 have lost, have you seen, haven't, did you last wear, wore, left 5 has just left, has been, has never bought 6 left, did he go, didn't see, went 7 served, did that war begin, began, lasted 8 did you vote, voted, wasn't, was, lost 9 did you like, liked, quarrelled, dismissed, were, was 10 didn't know, knew, have you known, have known 11 hasn't had, have been 12 did you hear, did, did you think 13 didn't know, were, have you been, have been, have you been, went 14 have you tried, tried, found, started 15 have you seen, has anything happened, have escaped 16 has Mary fed, fed, did she give, gave 17 have you known, have known, did he do, came, was 18 haven't seen, hasn't been, bought 19 has the plumber been, stayed, did he do, turned, emptied 20 have you been, have been, did you enjoy, took, did you win, came 21 has that been, has been, have written, has been 22 have just been, have you seen, haven't, haven't read, read, was, did Tolstoy write, wrote, did he write 23 brought, did he do, wanted 24 have you been, have been, did he take, did, did it hurt 25 said, hasn't phoned 26 have just received, haven't paid, didn't I give, did, spent/have spent 27 have you been, have just started, did you find, answered 28 have you finished, have done 29 have cut, did it happen, slipped 30 did you get, got 31 did you meet, did, had 32 lost, has been, did he lose, was 33 has been, did you see, happened, ran 34 phoned, got 35 did not wear, have worn

Exercise 19 1 have walked 2 have been walking/have walked 3 have been walking/have walked 4 have been making 5 have you made, have made 6 has eaten 7 hasn't stopped 8 has been drinking 9 have pulled 10 have been pulling 11 have you been doing, have been picking 12 have you picked, have picked 13 have slept 14 has been sleeping/has slept 15 has been riding 16 have ridden 17 has been making 18 have been working/have worked 19 have heard 20 have been hearing/have heard 21 have been greasing 22 have been polishing 23 have been working/have worked, has never said 24 has been teaching/has taught 25 have taught, have never met 26 have you been, have been pumping/have pumped 27 have pumped 28 have been looking/have looked, haven't found 29 has been coughing/has coughed 30 have you heard, have known 31 have been trying, have said 32 has been sounding 33 has been raining/has rained, has been postponed 34 has been hoping, hasn't dared 35 have been whispering, have you been helping, has he been helping 36 have you been making, have lost, have been trying, have been throwing

Exercise 20 1 for 2 for 3 since 4 for 5 for 6 since 7 since 8 since 9 for 10 since 11 for 12 for 13 for 14 for 15 since 16 since 17 for 18 since 19 for 20 since 21 since 22 since 23 for 24 since 25 since 26 since 27 for 28 since 29 since 30 for 31 for 32 since 33 for 34 for 35 for 36 since

2 Future and conditional tenses

Exercise 23 **be going to** is possible in all these sentences, but where the present continuous tense is given in the key, that is the better one to use.

1 am playing 2 is having 3 am going to light 4 are having 5 is being, are you putting, am putting 6 are you going, am going, am not buying/am not going to buy 7 am not going to do 8 am having 9 is coming, are you putting, am putting 10 is starting 11 am spending 12 is going to build 13 are you going to tell, am going to tell 14 is starting 15 is opening 16 is speaking 17 is closing 18 are you having, am having 19 am collecting 20 are taking 21 am giving 22 is singing 23 is going, is he flying, is going 24 is seeing 25 is he going to wash 26 is ringing 27 is going to ask 28 are giving, are inviting 29 is playing, is playing 30 are launching, are you coming 31 are you going to do 32 am picking 33 are you going, am

going, is calling 34 am competing 35 isn't coming 36 am going to read

Exercise 25 (**shall** can be replaced by **will** in these answers. Contractions may be used.)

1 shall recognize 2 will see/am seeing ('am seeing' implies a definite arrangement) 3 is playing 4 is coming 5 am going 6 shall know 7 shall owe 8 shall believe 9 am having 10 will have 11 is being/will be 12 is coming 13 is catching 14 are you meeting, am meeting 15 are you riding/will you ride 16 will Mrs Pitt say, won't mind 17 will it matter 18 won't forget 19 is leaving 20 shall remember 21 will break 22 will never forgive 23 will like 24 are laying 25 will see 26 will grow 27 will understand 28 will scratch 29 shall be 30 won't pass 31 is going 32 am moving 33 will soon forget 34 shall wait 35 won't write 36 will be

Exercise 26 (**shall** can be replaced by **will**. Contractions may be used.)

1 will go 2 will telephone 3 will send 4 am going to learn 5 are you going to do 6 will call, will translate 7 are you going to buy, am not going to eat, am going to eat 8 are you going to redecorate 9 am going to change, will help 10 are you going to put 11 am going to put 12 are going to do, am going to be 13 am going to shorten 14 won't lend 15 will cut 16 am going to attend 17 will ask 18 am going to open 19 won't read/am not going to read 20 will ask 21 am going to get 22 are you starting/are you going to start, am starting/am going to start 23 will make 24 are going to tow 25 am going to give up/am giving up 26 will say 27 will lend 28 are going to raffle 29 am going to put 30 will mend 31 will give 32 am going to make 33 am going to shorten 34 am going to buy 35 are you going to do 36 am going to give

Exercise 27 1 will you open 2 are you going to do/will you 3 are you going to paint 4 will you read 5 are you going to eat 6 aren't you going to climb 7 will you come 8 will you put 9 will you have 10 are you going to make 11 aren't you going to answer 12 will you come 13 are you really going to read 14 are you going to buy, will you buy 15 will you lend, are you going to fish 16 are you going to finish 17 will you give, are you going to make 18 are you going to leave 19 are you going to bath, will you help 20 will you drive 21 are you going to ride 22 are you going to eat 23 will you have 24 are you really going to call 25 are you going to paint 26 will you be ready 27 will you sit 28 will you do 29 will you be angry 30 are you going to work 31 will you call 32 are you going to walk 33 will you sign 34 are you going to give 35 are you going to explore 36 will you cook

Exercise 29 (**shall** can be replaced by **will** in these answers. Contractions may be used.)

1 will be walking 2 will walk 3 shall be bathing 4 will wash 5 shall be doing 6 shall be working/am working 7 will report 8 will be looking 9 shall be thinking/shall think 10 will assemble 11 will meet, will be wearing 12 will leave, shall be going/am going 13 will be debating/are debating 14 will go 15 will be working 16 will post, shall be going/am going 17 will be dancing/will dance 18 will be letting off . . . and making/will let off . . . and make 19 will remain 20 shall be sitting, won't be reading 21 will be going/will go 22 will be changing/will change 23 will come 24 will bring 25 shall all be living 26 will be going/will go 27 shall not be playing 28 will be opening/will open 29 will drive 30 shall be entering 31 will hand 32 will be arriving/will arrive 33 will be leaving/is leaving 34 will be using . . . and leaving/will use . . . and leave 35 will bring, will catch 36 will put

Exercise 30 (In these answers **I/we won't** can be replaced by **I am not going to/we are not going to** without any change in meaning. It is also grammatically possible to replace **you/he/they won't** by the **going to** form, but this would make the negative much less emphatic. **shan't** is replaceable by **won't**).

1 won't help 2 won't be meeting 3 won't cut 4 won't be cutting 5 won't be coming/isn't coming 6 won't come 7 won't lend 8 won't be speaking/isn't speaking 9 won't work 10 shan't be working 11 won't have 12 shan't be teaching/am not teaching 13 won't speak 14 shan't be writing 15 won't feed 16 won't go 17 won't paint 18 shan't be taking 19 won't borrow 20 won't wash 21 shan't be using 22 won't send 23 won't play 24 won't be singing/isn't singing 25 won't play 26 won't be taking part/isn't taking part 27 won't eat 28 shan't be eating 29 won't ride 30 won't be riding/isn't riding 31 won't give 32 won't be drinking 33 won't open 34 won't tell 35 won't eat 36 won't be wearing

Exercise 31 1 are you going to feed 2 are you letting/are you going to let/will you be letting 3 will you light 4 are you wearing/are you going to wear/will you be wearing 5 will you lend 6 will you come 7 will you have 8 are you having/are you going to have 9 are you going to study/will you be studying 10 will you be speaking 11 will you turn 12 Any one of the four forms is possible here: 'Will you take' implies that the matter has not yet been decided and that the speaker is offering a choice of dates. The other forms would imply that the matter has already been arranged and that the speaker is merely asking for information. 13 will you be listening/are you going to listen 14 will you help 15 will you come 16 will you lend 17 are you meeting/are you going to meet/will you be meeting 18 will you come 19 will you have 20 will you translate 21 will you be using/are you using/are you going to use 22 will you be going/are you going, will you get 23 will you come 24 will you be passing/are you going to pass/are you passing, shall be spending/am going to spend/am spending, will you get 25 are you going to keep 26 are you travelling/are you going to travel 27 are you going to repair 28 will you hold 29 are you going/will you be going 30 will you kindly explain 31 will you recognize 32 are you sending/are you going to send 33 will you tell 34 are you going/will you be going 35 are you going to type/will you be typing 36 will you look

Exercise 32 (Contractions may be used.)

1 shall/will 2 will 3 shall 4 shall 5 shall 6 shall 7 shall 8 will 9 shall 10 shall 11 shall 12 will 13 shall 14 will 15 will 16 will 17 will 18 shall/will 19 will, will 20 shall 21 will 22 shall 23 will 24 shall 25 will, shall/will 26 will 27 will 28 will 29 shall/will 30 shall/will 31 shall 32 will, will 33 will 34 shall 35 will, will 36 shall/will

Exercise 33 (**will** and **shall** may be contracted.)

1 returns 2 are 3 strikes 4 hears 5 shall/will have 6 comes 7 turn 8 gets 9 won't stop 10 goes 11 will see 12 will be 13 shall/will lend 14 will wake 15 will he ring 16 goes 17 is 18 shall/will give, comes 19 see 20 get 21 shall/will go 22 have 23 will fall 24 goes 25 begins 26 lifts 27 will continue 28 will become 29 won't move 30 will go on 31 learns 32 leap 33 shall/will have 34 get 35 begins 36 arrives

Exercise 35 (Contractions may be used.)

1 have taken 2 have finished/finish 3 have had 4 have been 5 goes/has gone 6 gets/has got 7 has done 8 have done 9 will see 10 have had 11 shall/will take 12 go 13 have seen 14 goes/has gone 15 won't let 16 shall/will let 17 sees 18 won't hear 19 has passed/passes 20 has sold 21 have swept/sweep 22 will get 23 will give 24 says 25 have returned/return 26 has been 27

have signed 28 won't know 29 have subsided/subside 30 has left 31 shall/will have 32 have had 33 shall/will stay 34 have made 35 has eaten 36 will come/come

Exercise 36 (**shall** can be replaced by **will**; both can be contracted.)

1 shall give 2 stand 3 will be 4 shall telephone 5 will arrest 6 will ruin 7 will steal 8 doesn't open 9 shall give 10 shall lend 11 don't go 12 shall be 13 is 14 hears 15 shall make 16 will bury 17 won't be 18 doesn't start 19 won't let 20 shall be 21 won't be 22 will you repay 23 rises 24 works 25 turns/will turn 26 catches 27 don't like 28 will have 29 see 30 will you promise 31 don't believe 32 will you buy 33 shall make 34 shan't be able 35 won't work 36 ring

Exercise 37 (**should** can be replaced by **would** in the following answers; both can be contracted.)

1 should type 2 should give 3 would look 4 wouldn't lose 5 wouldn't make 6 would come 7 were 8 would you visit 9 would you do 10 should buy 11 cleaned 12 would you be able/could 13 said 14 won 15 would you do 16 knew 17 should have 18 stopped 19 would not come 20 would you do 21 should be 22 wouldn't be 23 had 24 did 25 would grow 26 would fall 27 should keep 28 were/was 29 would be 30 should offer 31 got 32 would make 33 shouldn't go 34 would you spend 35 had 36 wasn't/weren't

Exercise 38 (**should** in the following answers may be replaced by **would**; contractions may be used in the affirmative and negative.)

1 should have visited 2 would not have been 3 had arrived 4 had been 5 should have been 6 had not seen 7 would have fallen 8 would you have accepted 9 would not have done 10 had known 11 should have offered 12 would not have stung 13 had realized 14 should have stopped 15 should have reached 16 should not have lent 17 had not sneezed 18 had put 19 would not have got 20 would not have tried 21 had spoken 22 would not have been 23 had known 24 had tried 25 would not have got 26 would not have put 27 had been 28 should have caught 29 would not have turned 30 had looked 31 would have been captured 32 had tried 33 should have taken 34 would have saved 35 had not called 36 would not have burnt

Exercise 39 (In the affirmative and negative **shall** and **should** can be replaced by **will** and **would** respectively; and contractions may be used. **should** in sentences 1, 7, 11 however does not change.)

1 find/should find 2 shall have 3 will happen 4 had had 5 will you stay 6 would you choose 7 gets/should get 8 comes 9 will sit 10 didn't talk 11 shall/should I do 12 had read 13 had 14 shall go 15 would you do 16 run 17 will not be 18 comes 19 would not have 20 had worn 21 leaves 22 will fall 23 don't change 24 should not have bought 25 hung 26 would be able to/could 27 should have brought 28 would have been 29 would not have printed 30 should not buy 31 want 32 won't be 33 would jump 34 would answer 35 had made 36 had known

3 Gerund, infinitive and participles

Exercise 41 1 do 2 sing 3 to swim 4 to live 5 to go, rain 6 say, understand 7 to see 8 repeat 9 use 10 ask, use 11 to get, start 12 remember 13 to do 14 to go, wait 15 leave 16 open 17 to wait 18 to smoke 19 (to) move 20 play 21 to accept 22 to arrive 23 know 24 wait 25 tell 26 send 27 go, to meet 28 to have 29 leave, want, to take 30 to go, make, go 31 go, to visit 32 to know, to live 33 not to inform, (to) disobey 34 come, stay 35 take, make, drink 36 to disappoint, let, have

Exercise 42 1 to be 2 wish to make 3 want, to know 4 remember, look 5 to learn, to know 6 to be 7 not to feed 8 see, to speak 9 to travel, to arrive 10 know, to use, show 11 to be 12 open/opening, move/moving 13 to make, believe 14 to have missed, go 15 shake/shaking 16 to try, to come 17 go, promise, not to tell 18 like to come, walk 19 to ask, to tell, to get 20 to put, (to) keep 21 to pay 22 show, to open 23 say, to say 24 to be 25 want, to tell, to call, to discuss 26 to give, see/be seeing, not to forget 27 open/opening, throw/throwing 28 to carry, help 29 to pick, to handle 30 crash/crashing, burst/bursting 31 to do, wait, to let 32 crow/crowing 33 tell, be, to check 34 come, go, be/have been 35 to learn 36 be, look

Exercise 44 (The following are possible answers. Other introductory verbs are often possible.)

1 He told her to put some coal 2 She told Tom to shut 3 I asked Mary to lend me her pen 4 I advised the boys not to read 5 He advised me not to believe everything I heard 6 asked me to fill up

the 7 I told them not to hurry 8 warned Mary not to touch the switch 9 told the bank clerk to put his hands up 10 begged me to do as he said 11 told Peter to help his mother 12 told the children not to make 13 told us to do whatever we liked 14 warned them not to miss their train 15 advised his client to read it before he signed it 16 asked her to sing it again 17 Robert's mother told him to brush his hair 18 advised him to buy 19 begged him not to drive 20 reminded his listeners to listen 21 asked her to come with him 22 advised her to cook it 23 warned the lady not to touch 24 told the boys not to argue with him 25 told him to pull as hard as he could 26 ordered the porter to send 27 advised us not to lend 28 told us to make a list of what we wanted 29 told her to look 30 warned the people on the platform to stand clear 31 asked me to see if I could find 32 warned her not to go 33 asked the customer to pay 34 told the children not to point 35 told the man to put the ladder 36 warned her to think well before she answered

Exercise 45 (Other introductory verbs and other indirect objects are usually possible.)

1 My father ordered me to come down at once 2 urged the country/ the people to be patient 3 advised the customer to buy the large tin 4 warned them not to bathe there 5 told the man to turn right 6 asked the customer to go 7 told the travellers to have their passports 8 ordered his men to stand 9 told the boy to translate 10 told her to listen 11 warned me not to believe everything she told me 12 ordered the crowd to keep moving 13 urged me to look 14 warned his son never to lend money to people he didn't know 15 asked the traveller to put his luggage 16 asked his patient to take 17 told him not to spend 18 invited me to tell her 19 told him to look around him 20 asked his mother to give him 10p. 21 asked the man to open his suitcases 22 always told us not to waste 23 asked me to pass 24 told his pupils/the class to dismount 25 asked Mary to put 26 advised her to come in 27 warned the children not to put their hands 28 told the boy not to lean his bicycle against his window 29 told the passengers to cross 30 asked me not to shout 31 asked her to meet him there . . . the following day 32 asked her not to decide . . . but to think 33 asked me to help her 34 told him to open 35 asked the mechanic to mend 36 warned her not to put

Exercise 46 1 too young to have 2 too cold to bathe 3 so kind as to answer/kind enough to answer 4 too old to wear 5 strong enough to support 6 enough money to live on 7 too furious to speak 8 hot enough to boil 9 foolish enough to tell/so foolish as to tell 10 thin enough to slip between 11 too ill to eat 12 too wide to get through 13 strong enough to dance on 14 too terrified to move 15 big enough to harm 16 strong enough to keep 17 too deep to wade 18 old enough to be 19 rich enough to buy 20 so good as to forward/good enough to forward 21 thick enough to walk on 22 too drunk to answer 23 too cold to have 24 rash enough to set off/so rash as to set off 25 high enough to see 26 old enough to understand 27 too snobbish to talk 28 too thick to push through 29 curious enough to open/so curious as to open 30 too impatient to remain 31 too clever to be caught 32 too dark to see 33 hot enough to fry 34 too bitter to eat 35 so kind as to turn down/kind enough to turn down 36 too cloudy to see

Exercise 47 1 to leave 2 only to find 3 You are to go 4 so kind as to lend/kind enough to lend 5 to mend/to be mended 6 to hear 7 for him to hear 8 It was stupid of me to be rude 9 to play with 10 for everyone to know 11 to sit 12 only to find 13 It was very brave of him to rush 14 to wear 15 He is expected to broadcast 16 to cook in 17 only to learn 18 to open it with 19 seems to have been committed 20 Is he likely to arrive 21 just about to leave 22 You are to be met 23 for them to have 24 He is said to have been 25 to continue the strike 26 kind enough to translate/so kind as to translate 27 for us to leave 28 It was stupid of you to sign 29 She is said to have 30 to swim 31 He is believed to be 32 He appears to have been killed 33 to realize 34 The earth is said to have been 35 only to discover 36 The murderer is said to be hiding

Exercise 48 (Brackets placed round **so as** or **in order** indicate that though it would be more usual to include these words it would be possible to omit them (see 308 B). Similarly in some of the other examples **so as** or **in order** could be inserted. This must not, however, be done in Nos. 5, 6, 17, or 24, nor in 15 unless the 'them' is retained (see 308 B). **so as** is interchangeable with **in order**.)

1 to paint 2 to remind 3 to feed 4 so as not to frighten 5 to put his savings in 6 to drink out of 7 to save 8 so as not to strain 9 in order to get 10 to tell 11 so as not to get 12 to frighten 13 so as not to make 14 to protect 15 to put on the fire 16 so as not to disturb 17 to study 18 in order to discuss 19 so as to be able 20 to elude 21 to prevent 22 to reduce 23 in order to read 24 to watch 25 in order to have 26 in order to keep 27 in order to learn 28 to buy 29 to warn 30 to avoid 31 to protect 32 so as to be able 33 to warn 34 to avoid 35 in order to look 36 so as not to alarm

Exercise 49 (**I/we would** is replaceable by **I/we should. would/wouldn't** in negative purpose clauses is usually replaceable by **should/shouldn't.** Where an infinitive phrase is possible the infinitive given in the key is not necessarily the only one that could be used.
To save space not more than two possible answers are given for any one example. Sometimes the **in case** construction would also be possible. **in case** can be followed by **should** + infinitive, though an ordinary present or past tense is more usual.)

1 so that nobody should/would know *or* to prevent anyone knowing 2 in case somebody knocks 3 so that repair work may/can continue *or* to allow repair work to continue 4 so that it wouldn't get broken *or* to prevent it getting broken 5 so that he wouldn't be recognized *or* to avoid being recognized 6 so that her fruit wouldn't be stolen *or* to prevent her fruit being stolen 7 so that I wouldn't overhear *or* to prevent my overhearing 8 in case you get bitten 9 so that the crew may/can escape *or* to enable the crew to escape 10 so that my children may/will have 11 so that the cows won't get *or* to prevent the cows getting 12 so that the call wouldn't be *or* to prevent the call being 13 so that the birds won't eat *or* to prevent the birds eating 14 in case there is 15 so that nobody will/can climb *or* to prevent anyone climbing 16 in case you have 17 so that the snow would/could slide 18 so that everyone may/will understand *or* to enable everyone to understand 19 so that anyone who finds him will/may know 20 so that the birds would know *or* to let the birds know 21 in case we are 22 so that the birds won't build *or* to prevent the birds building 23 in case he forgets 24 so that she wouldn't frighten *or* to prevent her frightening 25 in case the chimney catches 26 so that I couldn't/wouldn't be able to call *or* to prevent me calling 27 in case it is 28 so that young children won't be able to turn *or* to prevent young children turning 29 in case he breaks 30 so that the government may/can discuss *or* to let the government discuss 31 in case it is 32 so that pedestrians might/could cross *or* to let pedestrians cross 33 so that his secretary could/would be able to 34 in case they set 35 so that the rest of the party would know *or* to let the rest of the party know 36 so that the meat won't burn *or* to prevent the meat burning *or* in case the meat burns

Exercise 50 (**should** is replaceable by **ought to**.)

1 must have been 2 can't/couldn't have seen, must have dreamt 3 may/might have broken 4 needn't have carried 5 should have gone 6 were to have been 7 can't/couldn't have been, must have

been 8 shouldn't have eaten 9 may/might not have understood 10 needn't have given 11 must have escaped 12 shouldn't have lied 13 may/might have been, can't/couldn't have been 14 must have cooked 15 needn't have brought 16 must have told 17 was to have unveiled 18 may/might have been 19 must have met 20 should have done 21 can't/couldn't have caught 22 needn't have opened 23 must have betrayed 24 shouldn't have driven 25 could have climbed 26 would have asked 27 should have been abolished 28 shouldn't/needn't have boiled 29 was to have played 30 may/might have been 31 should have taken 32 must have had 33 may/might/could have fallen 34 must have been 35 needn't have translated 36 shouldn't have looked

Exercise 51 **(I'd** is replaceable by **I should. should** (obligation) is replaceable by **ought to** in numbers 5, 9, 13, 17. **may/might** in the affirmative is normally replaceable by **could.**

1 was to have married 2 needn't have repeated 3 seems to have been 4 were to have set out 5 shouldn't have eaten, may/might have been (**may** indicates that the danger is still present; **might** that it is over). 6 must have worked 7 needn't have brought 8 I'd like to have bathed/I'd have liked to bathe/I'd have liked to have bathed 9 should have written 10 wouldn't have come 11 must have been 12 may/might have been, can't/couldn't have been 13 needn't/shouldn't have bought 14 can't/couldn't have been 15 seems to have enjoyed 16 must have been 17 should have stood 18 was to have gone 19 I'd like to have photographed/I'd have liked to photograph/I'd have liked to have photographed 20 must have been 21 may/might have been 22 can't/couldn't have been driving 23 must have taken 24 may/might not have 25 I'd like to have gone/I'd have liked to go/I'd have liked to have gone 26 can't/couldn't have seen 27 may have been 28 may/might have been started 29 must have had 30 may/might have read, can't/couldn't have read, must have told 31 may/might have been waiting 32 must have misheard 33 might have borrowed 34 I'd like to have asked/I'd have liked to ask/I'd have liked to have asked 35 must have been 36 is said to have been

Exercise 53 1 seeing 2 having 3 to meet 4 to work 5 to see 6 waiting 7 not to touch 8 to lock, going 9 not to speak 10 behaving 11 to explain, to listen 12 smoking 13 to know 14 to disguise, dressing 15 to wait 16 showing, to work 17 walking, catch up 18 to understand 19 exceeding 20 playing, doing 21 to inform 22 overhearing 23 smoking, to smoke 24 going, saying 25 writing, waiting 26 to avoid being 27 giving, to speak 28 to persuade, to agree 29 cleaning, to do 30 shutting, sitting 31 sneezing, sitting 32 talking, to finish 33 to give up smoking 34 stopping, forgetting to wind 35 realizing, helping 36 to make, rubbing

Exercise 54 1 answering, ring 2 letting, chase, being 3 driving, being driven 4 to start looking 5 lending, to make 6 Lying, sitting 7 to go 8 neglecting to take 9 to show, to use 10 going, to see/seeing 11 telephoning, asking, to look 12 hearing, not to enter 13 to have, writing 14 to answer, replying 15 to pacify, to be pacified, grumbling 16 offering, to leave, (to) work 17 making, to do 18 having to get up 19 to forget, worrying 20 remaining, to help, to stay 21 to run, to have recovered 22 listening, hearing 23 to learn, reading, listening 24 to start, to wait 25 discussing, having reached 26 having, to ride 27 (to) leave, meeting, recognize 28 paying 29 to give 30 interrupting, repeating 31 cutting, to go 32 buying, selling 33 giving, to explain 34 asking, telling, to buy 35 to tell, looking 36 to be, to erupt/erupting

Exercise 55 1 to ride, to do, coming, to come 2 spending, earning 3 being, to apologize 4 to eat 5 working, spending 6 looking, being 7 posting 8 to lock, go, do 9 to learn, saying 10 trying to interrupt, to wait, talking 11 doing, to move/moving 12 leaving, to go 13 to drink 14 being, to wait 15 trying to make, adding 16 going, stay 17 to look, (to) take, looking, to do 18 getting up, walking 19 listening, listening 20 to make/making, to see 21 doing 22 to put, to prevent, climbing 23 taking, to eat 24 ringing, asking, to do 25 waiting, to clear, to set 26 repeat, to make, to do 27 leaving, sending, to tow 28 borrowing, asking, to do 29 to offend, annoying 30 to be able to tell, gazing 31 getting, to walk 32 to ask, to leave 33 setting, having been 34 to go 35 to go, (to) try to save, cutting 36 earn, scrubbing, make, blackmailing

Exercise 56 1 beginning to slip/begin to slip/begin slipping, to save, falling 2 falling, trying to keep 3 to lend, taking 4 to open 5 hearing, dropping, to realize 6 to book, to keep, to lose 7 to avoid being, being/to be, waiting 8 to get, to ask 9 making, speak/speaking 10 to win, cheating 11 firing/to fire, striking/strike 12 strike/striking, to get 13 ringing/ring, to be coming to open 14 to go, to give 15 to put, (to) watch, change/changing 16 to see, to avoid hitting 17 to be, crackling 18 climbing, to explain, to say, to let, go 19 convincing, to get, leap 20 driving, doing, to do 21 to sit, (to) hear, howling 22 getting, climbing, to do 23 roar/roaring, to move/ moving, waving 24 writing, to do, to go, see 25 walking, to cross, thinking, to chase 26 to be having, thudding 27 getting, to pay 28 to come, standing 29 to like making and flying . . . doing 30 to arrive, rising 31 sawing, fall/falling 32 to see/seeing, crying/ cry 33 jump/jumping, fall/falling 34 to wake, (to) hear, beating 35 beginning to roll/begin to roll/begin rolling, to do, to stop 36 laughing, slipping/slip

Exercise 57 1 Knowing that he was poor, I offered 2 Having barricaded the windows, we assembled 3 Becoming tired of my complaints, she turned it off 4 Finding/having found no one at home, he left 5 Hoping to find the will, she searched 6 Having removed all traces of his crime, he left 7 Realizing that he had missed the train, he began 8 Exhausted by his work, he threw 9 Having spent all his money, he decided 10 Having escaped from prison, he looked 11 Having heard the story before, she didn't want 12 Having found the treasure, they began 13 Entering the room suddenly, she found 14 Turning on the light, I was 15 Having visited the museum, we decided 16 Thinking we were lost, he offered 17 Having found his revolver and loaded it, he sat 18 Realizing that she couldn't move it alone, she asked 19 Having fed the dog, he sat 20 Addressing the congregation, he said 21 Thinking he had made a mistake somewhere, he went 22 Looking/having looked through the fashion magazines, I realize 23 The tree, uprooted by the gale, had fallen 24 People sleeping in the next room were 25 Knowing that the murderer was still at large, I was 26 Having stolen the silver, he looked 27 Soaked to the skin, we reached 28 Sitting/Seated in the front row, and using . . . I saw 29 One day, sitting by the fire, you will take 30 Knowing that the grass was very wet, I didn't like 31 Believing that she could trust him, she gave 32 Slates, ripped off by the gale, fell 33 The lion, finding his cage door open and seeing no sign of his keeper, left 34 The government, trying to tax people according to the size of their houses, once put a tax 35 Having heard that the caves were dangerous, I didn't like 36 Wearing extremely fashionable clothes and surrounded by photographers and press men, she swept

4 Auxiliary verbs

Exercise 61 (As mentioned in the note, the **do/did** form could be used throughout except in No. 27, and of course for the future.)

1 hasn't even (got) 2 has (got), has/has always got 3 don't have, have (got) 4 has (got) 5 haven't you (got) 6 did you have/had you 7 has

the alphabet (got) 8 do the houses have/have the houses (got) 9 have you (got), haven't (got) 10 do you ever have 11 he'll have 12 don't usually have 13 have you (got) 14 don't always have 15 hasn't your door (got) 16 have you (got), have 17 haven't (got) 18 has (got) 19 have you 20 has this desk (got), don't ever have/never have 21 do you ever have 22 do babies have 23 has/has a pentagon got 24 has, does she have 25 have, won't/don't have 26 do you have 27 have you (got), have (got) 28 have you (got), I only have/have only (got), will have 29 have you (got) 30 have you (got), have, haven't (got) 31 hasn't he (got) 32 have, didn't have/ hadn't 33 didn't you have 34 do red-haired people always have/ have red-haired people always got 35 hasn't (got) 36 have you (got)

Exercise 62 1 are having 2 did you have/had you 3 is having 4 are having 5 does he have, he usually has 6 do you have 7 do you have, have 8 do you have, have 9 don't you have 10 were having 11 did you have/had you 12 are having 13 will you have 14 am having 15 had 16 did you have 17 am having 18 are having 19 was having 20 do English people always have 21 don't have/haven't 22 are having 23 don't have 24 did you have/had you, had 25 did you have/had you 26 am having 27 does he have 28 did you have/had you 29 had 30 are having 31 didn't have/hadn't 32 are having 33 am having 34 is having 35 does he ever have 36 had, did you have/had you

Exercise 63 1 am having 2 am having 3 had 4 am having 5 had 6 am having 7 are having 8 does he have 9 do you have 10 don't you have 11 do you have 12 am having 13 have the grass cut 14 have it repaired 15 have it shortened 16 am having them typed 17 have it tuned 18 have it cleaned 19 had them dyed 20 have a puncture mended 21 have it set 22 have it (taken) out 23 am having it redecorated 24 had one built/are having one built 25 have my car greased 26 had it seen to 27 had my watch cleaned 28 am having my shoes repaired 29 they had the man arrested 30 he had the car towed 31 they had a new roof put on 32 have my windows cleaned 33 had my eyes tested 34 have them made 35 had the oysters opened 36 had my ears pierced

Exercise 64 1 is being/will be ruined 2 is to make/is making 3 were 4 being, being 5 were to be/should be extinguished 6 have you been 7 is being pulled down 8 was to put 9 isn't it 10 are to stay 11 should be asked 12 were to 13 I am to go 14 is being carried 15 to be 16 were 17 were to have taken 18 is being taught 19 was, will be, were 20 to be 21 was to have been 22 should be sent 23 will there be 24 had been 25 is to open/is opening 26 were being taken 27 was to have been 28 would you be 29 is to be/is being/will be 30 was to have run 31 was still being painted 32 should be printed 33 are being/have been translated 34 were 35 was to do 36 is to be

Exercise 65 1 can, could, can't/couldn't 2 will be able to 3 won't be able to 4 can't . . . can't *or* couldn't . . . couldn't 5 shall/will be able to 6 will never be able to 7 couldn't, can't 8 will you be able to 9 won't be able to 10 could, couldn't 11 can, can, can't 12 can't, can't/couldn't, can't/couldn't 13 could/was able to 14 was able to 15 could/was able to, couldn't/wasn't able to 16 were able to 17 were you able to/could you 18 couldn't/wasn't able to 19 was able to 20 were able to 21 could/was able to 22 was able to 23 was able to 24 was able to 25 could/can, could 26 could, couldn't 27 could, couldn't, can't 28 could 29 couldn't/wouldn't be able to 30 couldn't/wouldn't be able to 31 could/can, can't 32 could, could 33 could/can, couldn't/can't 34 couldn't/wouldn't be able to 35 couldn't/ wasn't able to, couldn't/wasn't able to 36 could

Exercise 66 1 may 2 might 3 may/might 4 may/might 5 might 6 may 7 may/might 8 might 9 may 10 may 11 might 12 may 13 may/might 14 may/might, may/might 15 might 16 may 17 may 18 may 19 may/might 20 might 21 might 22 may/might 23 may/might 24 may/might 25 might 26 may/might 27 might/ may 28 may/might 29 may 30 might 31 might 32 may/might 33 might 34 might 35 may/might 36 may/might

Exercise 71 1 – 2 to 3 to 4 to 5 – 6 to 7 to 8 – 9 – 10 to 11 to 12 to 13 (to) 14 – 15 – 16 –, to 17 to 18 to 19 – 20 – 21 to 22 to 23 – 24 to 25 – 26 to 27 –, (to) 28 – 29 – 30 to 31 – 32 to 33 to 34 – 35 to 36 to

Exercise 72 1 has to 2 must 3 has to 4 have to 5 must 6 have to 7 had to 8 has to 9 had to 10 have to 11 must 12 will have to/have to 13 must 14 has to 15 must/you've got to 16 have to 17 have to 18 must 19 must 20 have to 21 had to 22 must 23 have to 24 must 25 has to 26 must 27 will have to 28 must 29 had to 30 have to 31 will have to 32 had to 33 have to 34 must/will have to 35 must 36 have to

Exercise 73 (Add **not** to each of the following verbs.)
1 need 2 must 3 must 4 need 5 must 6 must 7 need 8 must 9 need 10 need 11 need 12 must 13 need 14 must 15 must 16

need 17 must 18 must 19 need 20 need 21 must 22 must 23 need 24 must 25 must 26 must 27 need 28 need 29 need 30 need 31 need 32 must 33 need 34 must 35 must 36 need

Exercise 74 (**didn't have to** is replaceable by **didn't need to**.)

1 he doesn't have/hasn't (got) to 2 did you have to 3 I don't have to 4 they will have to 5 we didn't have to 6 we didn't have to 7 you needn't come 8 I never have to 9 shan't/won't have to 10 you needn't 11 shall we have to 12 you don't have to 13 I didn't have to 14 we don't have to 15 have you got to/must you/need you 16 do people have to 17 shall I have to 18 don't have to 19 we didn't have to 20 women don't have to 21 we didn't have to 22 do we have to/must we 23 did you have to 24 I didn't have to 25 you won't have to 26 they didn't have to 27 do you have to/have you got to 28 did you have to/had you to 29 didn't have to 30 shall I have to 31 do you have to/have you got to 32 I didn't have to 33 do French children have to 34 did you have to 35 I didn't have to 36 did you have to

Exercise 75 1 must have been 2 can't/couldn't have been 3 needn't have helped 4 must have left 5 can't/couldn't have escaped 6 needn't have given 7 can't/couldn't have seen 8 must have started 9 can't have been 10 needn't have bought 11 must have been 12 must have borrowed 13 must have stolen 14 needn't have done 15 needn't have said 16 can't/couldn't have understood 17 can't/couldn't have done 18 must have been 19 can't/couldn't have walked 20 can't have been 21 must have been 22 can't/couldn't have had 23 needn't have watered 24 must have taken 25 can't/couldn't have been 26 can't/couldn't have watered 27 must have been 28 needn't have sent 29 needn't have made 30 must have been 31 must have been 32 can't/couldn't have seen 33 can't/couldn't have come 34 needn't have lent 35 needn't have spoken 36 must have fallen

Exercise 76 (**shall** is replaceable by **will** in Nos. 6, 11, 13, 28, 29, 34, 35.)

1 shall 2 will 3 shall 4 will 5 shall 6 shall 7 shall 8 will 9 will 10 shall 11 shall 12 will 13 shall 14 will 15 will 16 shall 17 will 18 shall 19 will 20 will 21 shall 22 shall 23 will 24 will 25 shall 26 will 27 shall 28 shall, will 29 shall 30 will 31 will 32 will 33 will, will 34 shall 35 shall, will 36 shall, will

Exercise 77 (**should** is replaceable by **would** in Nos. 6, 14, 26, 27, 30.)

1 would 2 would 3 should 4 would 5 would 6 should 7 should 8 would, would 9 should 10 would 11 should 12 would 13 would 14 should 15 should 16 would 17 should 18 would, would 19 should 20 would 21 should 22 should 23 should 24 should 25 should 26 should 27 should 28 would 29 should 30 would, should 31 should 32 should, should 33 would 34 should 35 should 36 should

Exercise 78 1 should, should 2 would 3 should 4 should 5 would, would, would, would 6 should 7 should 8 would, would 9 should, should/would 10 should 11 would 12 would, should 13 should 14 should 15 should, would 16 should 17 should 18 would, should 19 should 20 would 21 should 22 would 23 should 24 should 25 would, would 26 would 27 should 28 would 29 should 30 should, should, would 31 should 32 should 33 should/would, would 34 would, would 35 should 36 would, would

Exercise 79 (In Nos. 1, 7, 10, 20, 23 **should** is replaceable by **ought to**. **may** is replaceable by **might**.)

1 should have been 2 may have written, couldn't have written 3 must have fallen 4 may have liked 5 must have been 6 needn't have sent 7 might/should have left 8 may have been 9 can't/couldn't have been, may have been 10 shouldn't have gone 11 may have been 12 were to have been 13 should/would have been 14 needn't have carried 15 may have been 16 can't/couldn't have been, must have been 17 must have been 18 was to have been 19 would have reached 20 should have crossed 21 should have brought 22 may have been 23 must have been 24 can't/couldn't have been, must have been 25 may not have heard 26 could have put you up 27 would have fallen 28 should have checked 29 needn't have apologized 30 may not have realized 31 might/should have thanked 32 was to have gone 33 should have warned 34 would have known 35 needn't have bought 36 must have been

5 Indirect speech and passive voice

Exercise 80 (In many of these examples other pronouns would be equally correct.)

1 told her I had . . . to show her 2 said nothing grew in her garden . . . it never got 3 told his mother he was going away the next day 4 said

he had been . . . he hadn't had 5 remarked that it wasn't so foggy that day as it had been the day before 6 said that the underpass was being opened two days later 7 said they had moved into their flat but they didn't like it . . . their last one 8 said they had . . . it didn't work 9 said that . . . windows of his flat he could see 10 said she'd no idea what the time was but she'd dial 11 his wife had just been made 12 said she'd come with me . . . she was 13 said he had . . . that afternoon . . . he hadn't done his homework 14 warned her if she let . . . it would scorch her clothes 15 pointed out I hadn't given him . . . bill was . . . I'd paid him 16 Englishmen made . . . they were 17 she liked men . . . she didn't like them . . . She preferred . . . men looked silly 18 The report stated that the new Rolls Royce ran . . . all you could hear was . . . The Managing Director replied that they'd have 19 said she didn't know . . . her plums. She supposed (said she supposed) she'd have to . . . trouble was no one in her family ate 20 explained they liked working . . . they got 21 that he was . . . and he did all his own 22 told Joan she could keep that one if she liked as she had 23 said he was going fishing with his mother that afternoon and they were just going 24 told her she had got my umbrella and that hers was in her bedroom 25 explained to his client that he knew what they had said because he had put 26 said she'd sit up till she came in but she hoped she wouldn't 27 told me that if I gave him . . . he'd . . . for me 28 said she had . . . it didn't seem . . . to her weight

Exercise 81 (See note above key to Exercise 80.)

1 he hadn't been able to get . . . he had lost his key, so he had had to break 2 the mirror was there . . . he could see himself when he was dancing 3 she had written to him two days before and wondered why he hadn't 4 told the customer that it was quite . . . he used . . . himself 5 told me if he had spoken to his father as I spoke to mine/him, his father would have beaten him 6 told him that if he wanted . . . he'd better apply . . . *or* She advised him to apply early if he wanted . . . She had once tried . . . theatre had been booked out 7 they had walked . . . the previous night . . . protest about their rent. The Minister had been . . . had promised . . . what he could for them 8 said/threatened she would drop dead one day . . . he'd be sorry 9 her new house was supposed . . . she hadn't seen 10 says that he will wear his heart upon his sleeve 11 if it rained that afternoon it would be . . . the following day 12 told her guest she had meant . . . she had plugged . . . She was always doing 13 he had been intending . . . the next day . . . didn't think he'd be 14 told Mrs Smith that he was sure her son would do . . . he had done very well at the school 15 complained to/told her husband

that nothing she could do pleased his father. She (said that she) didn't think he liked her. Her husband answered that she mustn't think that; it was . . . he was old and found it 16 told her the steak was . . . and said/added that he was not complaining but was just pointing 17 reported that the burglars hadn't been able . . . had carried it 18 told me that if I saw her father I'd recognize him . . . He was 19 he had found . . . the day before . . . was going . . . that afternoon 20 he had got out . . . while he was standing . . . the gears (had) engaged . . . and the boat had gone/went 21 says he has done 22 said that if we arranged these/those slogans he might win 23 told me I might take his car if I liked and said he wouldn't be needing it the next day or the day after that 24 that the previous day Tom and she had gone/been to look . . . he was thinking . . . It was rather . . . and had a lovely garden but Tom had decided . . . was opposite 25 his wife wanted to take . . . he'd rather she concentrated on their home 26 she didn't know what my father would say when he saw . . . my puppies had made of the £5 note 27 it was high time I passed my test; she was tired 28 said that if he pressed his ear . . . he could hear . . . were saying

Exercise 82 (**if** is interchangeable with **whether** except in conditional sentences.)

1 asked why he was looking 2 asked who had put 3 asked which of them knew 4 asked why he had travelled 5 inquired how she could possibly run in her high-heeled shoes 6 asked them what their new house was like 7 asked where he was supposed to go 8 asked him whose car he had borrowed the previous night 9 asked me what she was/had been wearing when I saw her last 10 asked who owned the revolver 11 asked Mr M. where he had been the previous night 12 asked the boy what else he had seen 13 asked whether he had done that sort 14 asked her if she could read 15 inquired whether they had understood what I had said to them 16 asked the customer if he was being attended to 17asked him if he would go . . . the others did 18 asked Mary if she saw what he saw 19 inquired who had left 20 asked him if he had gone . . . and if he wanted 21 asked why his house was . . . and whether his father had been 22 asked if he was leaving that day or the following morning 23 asked how far it was and how long it would take 24 asked if he could speak to Mrs Pitt. The *au pair* girl answered that she was afraid she was out and asked if she could take 25 asked the little boy if he was sorry for what he had done 26 asked her if she was going to 27 asked the woman if she would mind if he looked inside her bag 28 asked the student if he would know what to do if someone fell at his feet

Exercise 83 (When it is not clear who is being addressed a first or third person pronoun is used in the answer. Other nouns or pronouns would of course be equally good.)

1 asked if I was going to let him in or if I wasn't 2 asked her if she had gone to France for her holidays or if she had stayed 3 asked what she was to do/should do with his mail while he was away and whether she was to/should forward it 4 asked (her) what she would wish for . . . appeared and offered her 5 wondered if he would ever understand 6 asked (me) if I would be there . . . and I said that I would 7 asked her doctor if she could lose/would be able to lose . . . He replied that she couldn't 8 wanted to know if she was to ask/should ask her to wait 9 asked viewers if they were not tired . . . and why they didn't . . . the firm's central heating 10 asked if I hadn't got a television set and I said that I hadn't and that nobody in our village had one. He asked me how I could bear 11 asked me if I wouldn't like to look . . . and I said that I wouldn't 12 asked if she should tell him what happened or if she should say . . . I asked her why she asked me and why she didn't ask 13 asked (him) if he had good . . . and if he suffered 14 asked (me) if I knew anyone in that area or if I could get . . . my previous 15 asked (him) if he had ever been convicted . . . and he said that he hadn't 16 The students were asked if they had/there were many . . . in their . . . and if they thought 17 asked (his uncle) if he thought the fog was going . . . and what they should do if it did. His uncle said that if it got worse they'd have 18 asked (me) if I'd like to see . . . or if I was 19 asked if I'd like to wait or if I'd rather come back the next day 20 He wondered if he would be 21 said he had just received his son's . . . and asked if I would like . . . I replied that I wouldn't 22 asked if she would be able to guide him or if he should bring 23 wondered if they would ever see 24 asked whether I stayed to the end or walked out in the middle when I didn't like a film 25 asked (me) what made me think that Smith was going to resign and if he had told me so or if I was only guessing and whether I would like 26 asked (me) if I found it stuffy/found the room stuffy and if he should open *or* offered to open 27 asked (me) if I had heard . . . that morning. I said that I had asked what it was/had been 28 asked her what animal she would choose to be if she had to be

Exercise 84 (See note above key to Exercise 83.)

1 told me to get out of his 2 ordered me to climb 3 asked the customer to pay 4 asked her to open her 5 told Mrs P. not to worry but (to) leave it all to him 6 advised him not to use 7 told the taxi-driver to follow the 8 recommended me to wash 9 urged me to

have confidence in him 10 told the lift-man to take him 11 advised the passengers to read 12 told her always to cook . . . and never to use 13 told him not to argue with his 14 whispered to me/told me not to make 15 told her to wait for him 16 advised her not to eat . . . and to avoid 17 advised me not to say 18 the notice told/asked people not to ask 19 told her not to forget 20 advised/told me to get my dog 21 asked him to write to her as often as he could 22 told him to put his 23 asked the porter to find him 24 told me not to forget my 25 told the children not to go 26 told his men to search 27 told her not to make 28 told him to put the gun down as it was loaded

Exercise 85 (See note above key to Exercise 83.)

1 advised us to make . . . our time as we wouldn't get 2 urged the public not to wait till the following day but to post . . . that day 3 warned them to be . . . and to remember that they drove/drive 4 said he couldn't open it and told/asked Peter to have 5 told me to go and get him . . . and to come 6 said someone was coming and told/urged me to get 7 warned us to give way to . . . the/our right 8 begged us to send whatever we could spare and said that . . . would be 9 advised him to wear a wig and said that then no one would know who he was 10 warned/told them not to bathe when the red flag was flying 11 told him not to forget/reminded him to thank . . . when he was saying 12 told me to watch . . . and not to let it 13 told/advised/warned me not to shelter . . . as the tree might 14 told me to put the message . . . and throw 15 told me to read it for myself if I didn't believe what he said 16 shouted to me to stop/told me to stop the dog as he had got her 17 told her husband not to drive . . . or the baby would 18 begged her to make . . . stronger and said that it had been . . . on the previous night 19 told me to do something and not just stand 20 told me to smell it and asked if I thought it had gone bad 21 told him not to take his coat off as they were going 22 told her to stand by the window and tell him if anyone went 23 told his pupil not to move till . . . waved him on 24 told me not to touch it as I would only make 25 warned her to be careful as the steps were 26 asked the girl to ask him to ring him back. The girl asked him to wait . . . and then to repeat the message 27 . . . told him to tell them not to work . . . as if they finished . . . they wouldn't get 28 The placard warned us to prepare to meet our doom as the end of the world was at hand.

Exercise 86 (See note above key to Exercise 83.)

1 told me to remember to get . . . when I was *or* reminded me to get, etc. *or* said that when I was at . . . I was to get 2 told/advised me to sit

down and put my head between my knees if I felt *or* said that if I felt faint I was to put/should put 3 asked what he was to do/should do with my purse if he found it. I told/asked him to keep it till he saw me 4 told me/asked me to give him a drink if he arrived before she got back *or* said that if he arrived before she got back I was to give 5 told me if anyone rang up to say *or* said that if anyone rang up I was to say 6 told me when I was driving always to look in my mirror *or* said that when I was driving I should always look 7 told me to leave the key under the mat if I went out *or* said that if I went out I was to leave 8 told me to shut the window if I thought the room was cold *or* said that if I thought the room was cold I was to shut/should shut 9 told me to ring him up if I felt lonely any time *or* said that if I felt lonely I was to ring 10 said that if she didn't want cabbage I was to ask her if she'd like (*the* **tell** *construction would be very clumsy here*) 11 told me to get the car off the road if I had a puncture and not to leave *or* said that if I had a puncture I was to get/should get . . . and not leave 12 told me to take the letter to the police if he wasn't back by that time the next day *or* said that if he wasn't back by . . . I was to take 13 told her husband not to forget/reminded him to thank Mrs Pitt when he saw her 14 told me to take the meat out of the oven when the bell rang *or* said that when the bell rang I was to take/should take 15 told them to give their . . . if they were taken . . . but to refuse to answer *or* said that if they were taken . . . they were to give . . . but (to) refuse 16 told them to shut . . . and go . . . when they heard *or* said that when they heard . . . they were to shut . . . and go 17 told me to press . . . if the lift should stop/stopped *or* said that if the lift should stop/stopped . . . I was to press/should press 18 told me to ask a client if he had a weak heart before I allowed him *or* said that before I allowed anyone . . . I was to ask/should ask

Exercise 87 1 suggested going/that they should go 2 urged his colleagues to show the nation that they were worthy of their 3 begged his mother to let him stay . . . that night 4 said he had worked for me . . . and suggested that I should give him 5 suggested leaving/that they should leave the wrecked car there . . . and said it might remind 6 told his pupil that he had helped him . . . up to then and suggested that he should try . . . by himself 7 said that no one was to speak to the man as he was 8 said that Tom had made the mess and that he was to clear 9 suggested that she should get herself *or* advised her to get 10 said he couldn't go with them that day but suggested their going/that they should go by themselves as it was 11 suggested giving a party but her husband was against the idea/opposed the idea 12 advised them not to jump . . . and suggested waiting until they heard . . . of the rumour *or* suggested that they shouldn't jump . . . but wait 13 advised her to stop/suggested that she should stop working and go . . . adding that she'd be *or* because she'd be 14 urged/exhorted the nations to forget . . . and to work 15 begged him to let her explain and asked him not to be 16 told the gardener to let the children play . . . if they wanted to adding that she was sure they wouldn't do 17 suggested staying there/that we should stay there till the storm had passed 18 grumbled that it was . . . and said that they should do

Exercise 88 1 said that if what she said was true he would have to go/must go 2 said that he had to/would have to/must be . . . the following day 3 asked if he had to make 4 told us that we mustn't come 5 told my nephew that his ticket would cost . . . he said . . . he would have to go . . . the next day 6 The park notice said that dogs must be kept 7 said that he must/would have to work 8 said that I needn't come in the following day and told me to take 9 said he had to/must go . . . the following day as he had 10 The notice said that passengers must not lean 11 said that there must be . . . because there was smoke 12 told him that when he was . . . he would have to tie his 13 said that port wine must never be shaken 14 said he hadn't had . . . and that he must be 15 said that the passport photo wasn't like her and that she must have/would have to have 16 told the children that they must not 17 said that I needn't/wouldn't have to/didn't have to get up till nine the next day 18 The railway regulations said passengers must be 19 asked (Tom) how he had got his dog . . . He/Tom said that he had carried him. I said that he must be 20 said that I mustn't/wasn't to tell anyone what she had just told me 21 asked (his mother) if he had to/need eat it all and she said that he must/had to 22 said that she had had to drive his pigs out of her garden 23 The notice said that sticks . . . must be left 24 asked her if she had to do it all that night or if she couldn't leave some for the following day 25 told me that when I went through Bayeux I must see 26 said that I must walk faster, I was far too slow 27 told me that I mustn't forget . . . or my friend would have to pay 28 said that he needn't tell me how grateful he was

Exercise 89 1 invited me to come/asked me to come/asked (me) if I would come . . . I thanked him and said that I'd love to 2 offered me another cup/asked me if I would like another cup. I thanked her and said that I wouldn't/thanked her and refused 3 The notice said that . . . an alarm bell would be rung and all passengers were to assemble 4 suggested ringing her up/that they should ring . . . as it was seven and she would be 5 told him to take the letters . . . and to shut the door as he went out 6 asked if I would help him or if he should ask someone 7 asked him to help her . . . as she couldn't lift it by herself 8 asked what she was to/should say if the client asked her where her employer was. Her employer told her to tell him that he had gone 9 wondered where they would all be 10 said that the milkman was . . . and asked if she was to/should pay him 11 said that she had broken the teapot Ann had given her . . . and asked what she should do. I advised her to try and get it mended 12 asked (me) if I would mind moving my car 13 asked what he was to/should do if he refused to let him in. I told him/advised him to write a note and push it 14 told him to be 15 asked (me) if I would mind cooking my own supper that night 16 asked me to look at the dreadful letter she had got and asked how she should answer it. I advised her not to answer/said that she shouldn't answer 17 The police asked anyone who had seen the accident to ring 18 The girl said that if I would sit/if I sat down the fortune-teller would be with me in a moment

Exercise 90 (The following are *possible* answers only; in most cases there are several alternatives.)

1 warned me not to walk on the ice as it wasn't safe 2 introduced Miss W. to Miss B. 3 gave him twenty pence and told him to go and get 4 begged him to do as I said 5 advised him to pretend to be 6 Tom offered to pay. Ann protested, but he insisted (on paying) 7 invited us to come in and look round, assuring us that there was 8 offered me a cigarette, which I refused *or* I thanked him and refused 9 cursed the map for leading him wrong 10 invited me to dinner the following night. I accepted with thanks/thanked him and accepted 11 asked him to show her how to work it, explaining that she wasn't 12 told her that she had pressed . . . and warned her not to do . . . as/or she might have 13 exclaimed with annoyance/disgust that he'd have to 14 suggested that the children should go 15 exclaimed delightedly/with delight that he had passed . . . I congratulated him 16 advised the young man always to be polite to people he passed . . . in case he met them again on his way 17 We wished him many happy returns of his birthday and he thanked us (for our good wishes) 18 complained to her children that they never listened to her and that it was . . . trouble she had had bringing them up 19 His wife welcomed him warmly/affectionately 20 urged him to eat up his . . . pointing out/assuring him that he would never grow . . . if he didn't eat 21 offered him £500 . . . his mouth 22 suggested waiting/that they should wait there till the rain stopped 23 cursed the zip-fastener for getting stuck 24 complained that if the boys did . . . he called them his sons, but if they did . . . he

called them hers 25 asked him if he knew that the shoes he was wearing weren't a pair. He replied that he did know but that he had been . . . that morning and those had been . . . he could/had been able to find 26 suggested going for a swim as it was quite fine 27 exclaimed with disgust that there was a slug . . . and summoned/called the waiter 28 called him a naughty boy (and scolded him) for fighting again. The boy protested that he hadn't started it, for the other boy had hit him first

Exercise 91 1 'Would he like to go to the concert?' she asked. 'I'm sure he would,' I said. 2 'Look where you are going,' she said to me; 'the road is full of holes and very badly lit.' 3 'While we were bathing,' they said, 'we saw someone examining our clothes.' 4 'Have you looked everywhere?' I asked. 'Yes,' she said. 5 'Let's give her/what about giving her a bottle of wine?' he said. 6 'The new carpet has arrived. Where am I to put/shall I put it?' he asked. 7 'An enormous load of firewood was dumped at my front gate two days ago. Since then I haven't been able to get my car out,' he said. 8 'Have some more wine?' they said. 'Yes, please,' I replied. 9 'If you find the front door locked, go round to the back,' he said to me. 10 'Who are you?' she asked the burglars, 'And who let you in?' 'Sit down and keep quiet,' they replied, 'unless you want to get hurt.' 11 'What was the weather like during your holidays?' he asked. 'It was awful,' I answered. 12 'Let's go down to the harbour and see/What about going down . . . and seeing if we can hire a boat?' he suggested. 13 'If you don't like escalators, you can go up the emergency staircase,' he told me. 'Thank you, I'll do that,' I said. 14 'What about Tom and you going ahead and getting the tickets?' *or* 'Suppose you and Tom go ahead and get the tickets?' he said to me. 15 'I think your electric iron is unsafe. I advise you to have it seen to' *or* 'I should have it seen to' *or* 'Why don't you have, etc.?' he said to me. 16 'If war breaks/broke out, I shall/should have to leave the country at once,' he said. 17 'Did you enjoy house hunting?' I asked him. 'No,' he said. 18 'I am surprised to see that the grandfather clock has stopped. Has anyone been fiddling with it?' she asked. 19 'I tried to ring up my mother several times yesterday, but I didn't succeed in getting through,' she said. 20 'Would you like to borrow this book?' I asked her. 'I have read it already, thank you, and didn't like it very much.' 21 'Are you going to the dance? Let's make up a party and go together' *or* 'What about making up a party and going together?' he said. 22 'Stop making a fuss about nothing,! You are lucky to have got a seat at all,' I told her. 23 'Do you want a single or a return ticket?' asked the clerk in the booking office. 'Is a return any cheaper?' I asked. 'It makes no difference,' he said. 24 'I hope you won't be offended,' my employer said, 'if I tell you that in my opinion you would do better in some other kind of job.' 25 'If your wheels had gone a couple of inches nearer the edge, madam,' said the A.A. man, 'the car would have plunged into the ravine.' 26 'You mustn't mind if the first one isn't any good,' he said to me. 27 'Do you think I am a liar?' he asked the crowd. 'Yes!' they shouted. 28 Stopping a man in the street, I asked, 'Would/could you help me with my car?' 'Would/will it take long?' asked the man. 'I'm on my way to catch a train.'

Exercise 92 1 wine should be opened . . . before it is used 2 steps had been cut and a rope fixed 3 my shoes had been cleaned and my suit brushed 4 room is used 5 nails must not be hammered 6 pigs are used 7 a light was switched on and the door opened 8 picture had been slashed 9 theatre is being pulled down 10 wasn't the roof mended 11 All the shop windows were broken 12 system was being started because books were not being returned 13 each of us was asked 14 refreshments will be served 15 bicycles must not be left 16 books may be kept . . . they must be returned 17 hole had been cut 18 it is being delivered 19 he has already been told 20 bells were rung 21 nothing can be done unless we are given more 22 far more is being spent on food now than was spent 23 paintings will be exhibited 24 nothing more will be said . . . if the . . . gun is returned 25 he was told 26 My dog was stolen and brought back only when £20 reward was offered. 27 he was given two weeks 28 flowers are made

Exercise 93 1 seals are fed 2 who was it written by? 3 compare clothes washed by us with clothes washed by any other 4 he expected to be offered 5 she was shown 6 oak was struck by lightning 7 it couldn't have been painted by T. because that kind of dress wasn't worn 8 she was stung by a jellyfish 9 special edition for . . . has been written 10 herbs used to be carried by judges 11 what was it written with? It was written with 12 shot was succeeded by an uneasy silence 13 were you interested by the idea? 14 he was given details 15 dams are made by beavers 16 engines used to be started by hand, now they are started by electricity 17 this was opposed by most people 18 a lot of the work is being done by students 19 dock was to have been opened by the P.M. 20 he is to be court-martialled 21 a lot of men will be made redundant by the closure 22 instructions could be understood by anyone 23 children . . . will not be admitted 24 ship is to be manned by boys 25 camp was flooded by a rainstorm 26 He was kept awake all night by the howling 27 It is thought that science should be taught by a scientist but that history can be taught by any idiot 28 All this damage couldn't have been done by children

Exercise 94 1 troops have been called out 2 trains were held up by fog 3 this is to be left here. It will be called for 4 police were called in 5 children were not properly looked after 6 reinforcements are being flown in 7 men of 28 were called up 8 he was looked up to by everyone 9 he will be seen off at the airport by all the ministers 10 bed hasn't been slept in 11 more rooms can be built on 12 he was thrown out 13 different attitude will have to be adopted 14 he ought to be locked up 15 they weren't taken in by her story 16 house was broken into 17 small plastic toys are being given away 18 notice was taken down 19 smoking is frowned on 20 after a million pounds had been spent the scheme was given up 21 my car had been towed away. I asked why this had been done and was told that . . . it had been parked 22 weapons must be handed in 23 he was shouted down 24 he is often taken for his brother 25 the cork hasn't been taken out 26 pool was to have been used . . . it is being filled in 27 students are being turned away 28 sky-scraper will have to be pulled down as the town planning regulations have not been complied with

Exercise 95 1 money was added up and found to be correct 2 this engine is claimed to be 3 a terrible mistake seems to have been made 4 you are supposed to make tea 5 he is known to be armed 6 he was seen to pick up 7 you are known to have been 8 he is believed to have 9 this needn't have been done 10 you had better have it taken in 11 he likes to be called 'sir' 12 this switch isn't to be/mustn't be touched 13 you will have to have/get it seen to *or* it will have to be seen to 14 this can't be done 15 we are being followed 16 boys used to be made to climb 17 it has to be seen to be believed 18 I am tired of being ordered about 19 he doesn't like being laughed at 20 this watch needn't be wound/doesn't need to be wound 21 he shouldn't have been told 22 rocket is said to have travelled . . . and to have landed 23 he is believed to have been killed 24 letters are to be sent 25 she is considered to have been 26 smoking is not allowed 27 the expedition is known to have reached 28 before printing was invented everything had to be written

Exercise 96 1 why don't you get an oculist to test your eyes? 2 the authorities are to introduce this . . . limit 3 they are lengthening the runways 4 nurses are wakening patients 5 people say/it is said that B. lived 6 British fishermen must offer any sturgeon that they catch to the Queen 7 someone has tampered with this signpost 8 squatters have been using their houseboat 9 they were towing the . . . ship 10 get a builder to put in a lift 11 The firm made a profit . . . but a loss of . . . which they made . . . cancelled this 12 guests will wear evening dress 13 the authorities put the ship . . . and forbade passengers and crew 14 we shall have to find someone 15 the police made him walk along . . . and repeat 16 our opponents must have started 17 the New Arts Gallery is to exhibit my paintings 18 experts have proved that this scientific theory is false 19 they are to salvage the car which the wind blew 20 police are guarding the house where they found the dead man to prevent anyone from entering it and interfering with the evidence 21 why didn't you either lock the car or put it 22 people are saying that the government is spending too little money 23 you could put your money to good use instead of leaving it idle 24 people believed that the earth was flat 25 no one has read this copy; no one has cut the pages 26 the police led away the student who threw the stones 27 people say that early E. and G. sailors used carrier pigeons 28 a strong police guard was escorting the referee

Preface to the New Edition

This is one of two books of exercises designed to accompany *A Practical English Grammar.*

The exercises in Book 1 are graded 'A', 'B' and 'C'. 'A' means difficult, 'B' means moderately difficult and 'C' means easy. These gradings are printed at the head of each exercise. In Book 2 all the exercises are of an intermediate difficulty and have not therefore been graded by letters in this way.

Some of the exercises are in the form of a dialogue between two people. Quotation marks are not used here but the second remark is usually printed directly below the first. Where both remarks are very short, they sometimes follow each other on the same line with a space between them.

Keys to most of the exercises are supplied in separate booklets. It has not been felt necessary to provide keys for every exercise.

It will be noticed that in some places the old imperial weights and measures have been retained, in others they have been replaced by metric ones. This is deliberate, as both forms are in daily use among English speakers.

Contents

1 Present and past tenses

1 Auxiliary verbs

C PEG 102–3

Read the following
a in the negative
b in the interrogative
c in the third person singular
(Auxiliaries are used both by themselves and as part of various tenses of ordinary verbs.)

Note
1 **may** for 'possibility' cannot be used in the interrogative at the beginning of a sentence. Instead we use a phrase such as 'Do you think that' + a future tense, or 'Is it likely' + an infinitive.

e.g. No. 1 Am I likely to see him?
No. 13 Do you think that they will come?

2 Use **needn't** as the negative of **must** in Nos. 15, 23, and 30.

1 I may see him.
2 They should read more.
3 You are six feet tall.
4 We are seeing Mary tomorrow.
5 They can play the guitar.
6 The girls are playing tennis.
7 We can tell you the time.
8 The birds are eating the buds.
9 I can show him the way.
10 They have a house.
11 My boss will be angry.
12 Tom and Ann can go by bus.
13 They may come tonight.
14 We are cleaning our own shoes.
15 They must obey me.
16 The boys have seen the comet.
17 These lakes are deep.

18 These exercises are all wrong.
19 They are very cold.
20 They may (*permission*) take the car.
21 They have made a cake.
22 These nests are made by wasps.
23 You must be quick.
24 Their gardens are full of weeds.
25 They are in a hurry.
26 You have a lot of grey hairs.
27 I am ashamed.
28 You'll be able to drive in a few days.
29 They have written to him.
30 We must lend him some money.
31 The cows are walking on the daffodils.
32 These plays are written by the students.
33 They will be ill if they eat it.
34 These repairs will take a long time.
35 Some pearls are made by oysters.
36 I have a bad cold.

2 Auxiliary verbs

C PEG 102–3

Put the following verbs into the past tense. (Auxiliaries are used both by themselves and as part of certain forms and tenses of ordinary verbs.) Use **had to** as the past tense of **must**.

1 He isn't working hard.
2 She doesn't like cats.
3 I can't say anything.
4 We must read it carefully.
5 I am afraid of cows.
6 He can lift it easily.
7 It isn't far from London.
8 Isn't it too heavy to carry?
9 He is mowing the grass.
10 He hopes that Tom will be there.
11 How much does this cost?
12 They haven't much money.
13 How old is he?
14 Do you see any difference?

15 I do what I can.
16 How far can you swim?
17 You must change that.
18 Tom can always ride my bicycle.
19 What time is it?
20 Have you time to do it?
21 Are you frightened?
22 Must you pay for it yourself?
23 What have you got in the box?
24 We hope that he'll come.
25 He says that she may not be in time. (He said that she . . .)
26 Do you understand what he is saying? I don't.
27 There are accidents every day at these crossroads.
28 She thinks that it may cost £100. (She thought that it . . .)
29 Doesn't Mr Pitt know your address?
30 They aren't expecting me, are they?
31 He thinks that the snakes may be dangerous. (*see 28*)
32 She wants to know if she may borrow the car. (She wanted to know if . . .)
33 Is she interested in crocodiles?
34 Tom is certain that he will win.
35 Can you read the notice? No, I can't.
36 I don't think that the bull will attack us.

3 Auxiliary verbs

C PEG 104

Answer the following questions
a in the affirmative
b in the negative

in each case repeating the auxiliary and using a pronoun as subject.

e.g. Do you need this? Answer: Yes, I do. No, I don't.
Can Tom swim? Answer: Yes, he can. No, he can't.

Use **needn't** as the negative of **must**.

1 Is the water deep?
2 Do you know the way?
3 Can you swim?
4 Does he come every day?

5 Are you afraid of ghosts?
6 Are you feeling better?
7 Must you go?
8 Are you enjoying this?
9 Does he know you?
10 Are your neighbours noisy?
11 May I borrow your car?
12 Is English difficult?
13 Will she see him?
14 Do you play cards?
15 Should I tell the police?
16 Can you cook?
17 Are you Mr Pitt?
18 Did she sing well?
19 Is your name Pitt?
20 Were they frightened?
21 Will his mother be there?
22 Ought I to get a new hat?
23 Should I marry him?
24 Was the driver killed?
25 Have you any money?
26 Did you dismiss him?
27 Do you live here?
28 Should we cut the grass?
29 Is he happy?
30 Is it cold today?
31 Can I help you?
32 Must you type it?
33 Are you having a bath?
34 Am I in your way?
35 Does he love you?
36 Are you hungry?

4 The simple present tense

C PEG 168–9

Read the following in the third person singular. Do not change the object if it is plural.

1 I think I am right.
2 Policemen often direct traffic.

3 They help their father.
4 Butchers sell meat.
5 We live in London.
6 They worry too much.
7 You drive too quickly.
8 I always carry an umbrella.
9 Why do dogs bark?
10 His sons go to the local school.
11 Cats don't bark.
12 Buses go every ten minutes.
13 I always read the *Guardian*.
14 Do you like boiled eggs for breakfast?
15 These seats cost £2.
16 I go to church on Sundays.
17 Elephants never forget.
18 You make very bad coffee.
19 Do ducks lay big eggs?
20 I often forget my own age.
21 Do you like snails?
22 Do you often eat garlic?
23 I cook my own meals.
24 Englishmen seldom speak at breakfast.
25 Detectives don't wear uniform.
26 What do they do?
They do nothing. They lie in bed all day.
27 Good children always obey their parents.
28 They kiss their mother when they come home from school.
29 Englishmen rush home when the day's work is over.
30 The boys box in the gymnasium on Fridays.
31 His dogs always attack strangers.
32 These hotels don't allow dogs.
33 Motor cycles don't make a lot of noise.
34 I brush my hair every night.
35 My hens often fly over the wall and lay eggs in Mr Pitt's garden.
36 They do exercises every morning before breakfast.

5 The simple present tense

C PEG 168–9

Read the following
a in the negative
b in the interrogative.

In Nos. 2 and 14, **have** is used as an ordinary verb and should be treated as one.

1 You know the answer.
2 He has breakfast at 8.00.
3 Jack loves Jill.
4 Some schoolgirls wear uniforms.
5 He trusts you.
6 It melts in the sun.
7 The bell rings at 8.00.
8 The flowers look fresh.
9 Those children like sweets.
10 He thinks too much.
11 He lives beside the sea.
12 They talk in their sleep.
13 This stove heats the water.
14 She has a cold bath every day.
15 Climbers often carry ropes.
16 He usually believes you.
17 He sows seeds in the spring.
18 I remember the address.
19 She plays chess very well.
20 They always forget to pay.
21 These thieves usually work at night.
22 He leaves home at 8.00 every day.
23 Most men shave every day.
24 She agrees with you.
25 Their dogs bark all night.
26 Their neighbours often complain.
27 Tom enjoys driving at night.
28 They feel very cold.
29 Tom looks very well.
30 They sell fresh grape juice here.
31 She spends all her money on clothes.
32 She cuts her husband's hair every week.

33 They pick the apples in October.
34 The last train leaves at midnight.
35 This car breaks down frequently.
36 That planet moves round the sun.

6 The present continuous tense

C PEG 160–4

Put the verbs in brackets into the present continuous tense. In No. 25, **have** is used as an ordinary verb and can therefore be used in the continuous tense.

1 She (not work), she (swim) in the river.
2 He (teach) his boy to ride.
3 Why Ann (not wear) her new dress?
4 The aeroplane (fly) at 2,000 metres.
5 What Tom (do) now? He (clean) his shoes.
6 This fire (go) out. Somebody (bring) more coal?
7 It (rain)?
Yes, it (rain) very hard. You can't go out yet.
8 You (mend) my shirt.
9 You (not tell) the truth.
How do you know that I (not tell) the truth?
10 Who (move) the furniture about upstairs?
It's Tom. He (paint) the front bedroom.
11 Mrs Jones (sweep) the steps outside her house.
12 What you (read) now? I (read) *Crime and Punishment*.
13 It is a lovely day. The sun (shine) and the birds (sing).
14 Someone (knock) at the door. You (not go) to answer it?
I (go) in a minute. I just (get) out of my bath.
15 She always (ring) up asking silly questions.
16 My mother doesn't usually make cakes on Mondays, but she (make) one today as my aunt (come) to tea tomorrow.
17 Where is Tom? He (lie) under the car.
18 Can I borrow your pen or you (use) it at the moment?
19 You (do) anything this evening? No, I'm not.
Well, I (go) to the cinema. Would you like to come with me?
20 Child: Come and look. The house across the road is on fire!
Mother: I can't come now, I (make) an omelette. Is the Fire Brigade there?

Child: Yes, they have just arrived and the men (jump) down from the engine.

21 Mother: What the people of the house (do)?
Child: Some of them (stand) in the street holding a blanket and others (throw) things down from the windows.

22 A woman (wave) from the attic. I think she is trapped. Perhaps the stairs (blaze).

23 The firemen (put) up a ladder, and one of them (climb) up to help her.

24 Now the fireman (come) down again. He (carry) a baby. The woman (follow).

25 We (have) breakfast at 8.00 tomorrow because Tom (catch) an early train.

26 Why you (type) so fast? You (make) a lot of mistakes.

27 What is the strange smell?
The people next door (cook) cabbage.

28 Tom usually feeds the hens but I (do) it today as he isn't well.

29 You can't see Ann because she (rest). She always rests after lunch.

30 They (dig) an enormous hole just outside my gate.
Why they (dig) it?
I don't know. Perhaps they (look) for oil.

31 What (make) that terrible noise?
It's the pneumatic drill. They (repair) the road.

32 The children are very quiet. Go and see what they (do).
They (cut) up some £5 notes.

33 What you (wait) for?
I (wait) for my change; the boy just (get) it.

34 I can't hear what you (say); the traffic (make) too much noise.

35 She always (lose) her glasses and asking me to look for them.

36 Why you (hide) the bottles?
I (hide) them because my mother-in-law (come) to dinner tomorrow and she doesn't approve of drink.

7 The simple present and the present continuous

B PEG 160–71

Put the verbs in brackets into the simple present or the present continuous tense.

1 Cuckoos (not build) nests. They (use) the nests of other birds.

2 You can't see Tom now: he (have) a bath.

3 He usually (drink) coffee but today he (drink) tea.
4 What she (do) in the evenings?
She usually (play) cards or (watch) TV.
5 I won't go out now as it (rain) and I (not have) an umbrella.
6 The last train (leave) the station at 11.30.
7 He usually (speak) so quickly that I (not understand) him.
8 Ann (make) a dress for herself at the moment. She (make) all her own clothes.
9 Hardly anyone (wear) a hat nowadays.
10 I'm afraid I've broken one of your coffee cups.
Don't worry. I (not like) that set anyway.
11 I (wear) my sunglasses today because the sun is very strong.
12 Tom can't have the newspaper now because his aunt (read) it.
13 I can't answer the phone now because I (paper) the sitting room walls.
14 The kettle (boil) now. Shall I make the tea?
15 You (enjoy) yourself or would you like to leave now?
I (enjoy) myself very much. I (want) to stay to the end.
16 How you (get) to work as a rule?
I usually (go) by bus but tomorrow I (go) in Tom's car.
17 Why you (put) on your coat?
I (go) for a walk. You (come) with me?
Yes, I'd love to come. You (mind) if I bring my dog?
18 How much you (owe) him? I (owe) him £5.
You (intend) to pay him?
19 You (belong) to your local library? Yes, I do.
You (read) a lot? Yes, quite a lot.
How often you (change) your books? I (change) one every day.
20 Mary usually (learn) languages very quickly but she (not seem) able to learn modern Greek.
21 I always (buy) lottery tickets but I never (win) anything.
22 You (like) this necklace? I (give) it to my daughter for her birthday tomorrow.
23 I won't tell you my secret unless you (promise) not to tell anyone.
I (promise).
24 You always (write) with your left hand?
25 You (love) him?
No, I (like) him very much but I (not love) him.
26 You (dream) at night?
Yes, I always (dream) and if I (eat) too much supper I (have) nightmares.
27 Who (whistle)? It is Mr Pitt. He (feel) happy.

28 These workmen are never satisfied; they always (complain).
29 We (use) this room today because the window in the other room is broken.
30 He always (say) that he will mend the window but he never (do) it.
31 You (know) why an apple (fall) down and not up?
32 You (write) to him tonight?
Yes, I always (write) to him on his birthday. You (want) to send any message?
33 Tom and Mr Pitt (have) a long conversation. I (wonder) what they (talk) about.
34 You (believe) all that the newspapers say?
No, I (not believe) any of it.
Then why you (read) newspapers?
35 This car (make) a very strange noise. You (think) it is all right?
Oh, that noise (not matter). It always (make) a noise like that.
36 The fire (smoke) horribly. I can't see across the room.
I (expect) that birds (build) a nest in the chimney. They always (do) that.
Why you (not put) wire across the tops of your chimneys?
We do sometimes but the birds usually (remove) it.

8 The simple present and the present continuous

B PEG 160–71

Put the verbs in brackets into the simple present or present continuous tense.

1 What Tom (think) of the Budget?
He (think) it most unfair.
I (agree) with him.
2 What this one (cost)? It (cost) forty pence.
3 You (hear) the wind? It (blow) very strongly tonight.
4 You (see) my car keys anywhere?
No, I (look) for them but I (not see) them.
5 He never (listen) to what you say. He always (think) about something else.
6 This book is about a man who (desert) his family and (go) to live on a Pacific island.
7 You (understand) what the lecturer is saying?
No, I (not understand) him at all.

8 What you (have) for breakfast usually?
I usually (eat) a carrot and (drink) a glass of cold water.

9 When the curtain (rise) we (see) a group of workers. They (picket) a factory gate.

10 Why you (walk) so fast today? You usually (walk) quite slowly.
I (hurry) because I (meet) my mother at 4 o'clock and she (not like) to be kept waiting.

11 I (wish) that dog would lie down. He (keep) jumping up on my lap.
I (think) he (want) to go for a walk.

12 You (recognize) that man?
I (think) that I have seen him before but I (not remember) his name.

13 My mother hopes that Jack (not come) to the party because he always (get) drunk.

14 This telegram has just arrived and the man (wait) in case you (want) to send a reply.

15 Stop! You (not see) the notice?
I (see) it but I can't read it because I (not wear) my glasses. What it (say)?
It (say) 'These premises are patrolled by guard dogs'.

16 She always (borrow) from me and never (remember) to pay me back.

17 You (need) another blanket or you (feel) warm enough?

18 It (save) time if you (take) the path through the wood?
No, it (not matter) which path you take.

19 I (save) up because I (go) abroad in July.

20 I (think) it is a pity you don't take more exercise. You (get) fat.

21 The plane that you (look) at now just (take) off for Paris.

22 Tom never (do) any work in the garden; he always (work) on his car.

23 What he (do) to his car now? I (think) he (polish) it.

24 That film (come) to the local cinema next week. You (want) to see it?

25 How Peter (get) on at school?
Very well. He (seem) to like the life.

26 Why Mrs Pitt (look) so angry?
Mr Pitt (smoke) a cigarette and (drop) the ash on the carpet.

27 This is our itinerary. We (leave) home on the 8th, (arrive) in Paris on the 9th, (spend) the day in Paris, and (set) out that night for Venice.
That (sound) most interesting. You must tell me all about it when you (get) back.

28 This story is about a boy who (make) friends with a snake which he (find) in his garden. Then he (go) away but he (not forget) the snake and some years later he (return) and (look) for it.

29 He (find) the snake who (recognize) its old friend and (coil) round him affectionately. But, unfortunately, the snake is by now a full-grown boa-constrictor and its embrace (kill) the poor boy.
30 The snake (feel) sorry about this?
I (not know). The story (end) there.
31 How you (end) a letter that (begin), 'Dear Sir'?
I always (put), 'Yours truly', but Tom (prefer) 'Yours faithfully'.
32 What the word 'catastrophe' (mean)?
It (mean) 'disaster'.
33 What you (wait) for?
I (wait) for the shop to open.
But it (not open) till 9.00.
I (know) but I (want) to be early, as their sale (start) today.
34 Why you (smoke) a cigar, Mrs Pitt? You (not smoke) cigars as a rule.
I (smoke) it because I (want) the ash. Cigar ash mixed with oil (remove) heat stains from wood.
35 Who (own) this umbrella?
I (not know). Everybody (use) it but nobody (know) who (own) it.
36 You (mind) if I (ask) you a question?
That (depend) on the question.
It (concern) your brother.
I (refuse) to answer any question about my brother.

9 The simple past tense

C PEG 172–3

Put the verbs in the following sentences into the simple past tense.

1 I go to work every day.
2 I meet her on Tuesdays.
3 He always wears black.
4 I make the cakes.
5 She gets up at 6.30.
6 He understands me.
7 They have lunch at 1.00.
8 She speaks slowly.
9 He leaves the house at 9.00.
10 I read a chapter every night.
11 You eat too much.
12 He often falls.

13 Tom sings very well.
14 He cries when he is hurt.
15 Who knows the answer?
16 He takes the dog out twice a day.
17 The curtain rises at 8.00.
18 I smoke 100 cigarettes a week.
19 We eat them raw.
20 I dream every night.
21 Bluetits often lay eggs in that nesting box.
22 He often feels ill.
23 I know what he wants.
24 I usually pay him 50p.
25 His dog always bites me.
26 I change my library book every week.
27 It costs 30p.
28 He signs the cheques.
29 I lie down after lunch.
30 We drink water.
31 His roses grow well.
32 I hate him.
33 I see him every day.
34 These dogs always fight.
35 I sometimes try to separate them.
36 He sleeps badly.

10 The simple past tense

C PEG 172–3

Put the verbs in the following sentences into
a the negative
b the interrogative.

1 I saw your brother.
2 We heard a terrible noise.
3 He slept till 10.00.
4 He looked at the picture.
5 They drank all the wine.
6 They set out for Rome.
7 She thought about it.
8 The police caught the thief.
9 He dug a deep hole.

10 She found her watch.
11 His nose bled for ages.
12 My mother chose this hat.
13 I lent you 20p.
14 She knelt on the floor.
15 Tom worked very hard.
16 He broke his arm.
17 His wife came at 8.00.
18 He lost his wallet.
19 His son wrote a poem.
20 We flew to New York.
21 Ann drew a map.
22 The duck laid an egg.
23 Mr Pitt fell downstairs.
24 She lost her way.
25 He forbade her to leave.
26 I sent it to the laundry.
27 Jack kept the money.
28 He rode slowly.
29 I spent £5.
30 She sold the car.
31 Jean rang the bell.
32 The sun rose at 6.00.
33 The boys ran home.
34 Mr Pitt shook the bottle.
35 He forgave her.
36 Mrs Pitt translated it.

11 The past continuous tense

C PEG 175

Put the verbs in brackets into the past continuous tense.

1 Detective, 'I'm afraid I must ask you both what you (do) yesterday at 10.20 p.m.'
Mr X, 'I (play) chess with my wife.'
Mr Y, 'I (listen) to a play on the radio.'
2 The children were frightened because it (get) dark.
3 It was a fine day and the roads were crowded because a lot of people (rush) to the seaside.

4 The aeroplane in which the football team (travel) crashed soon after taking off.
5 He usually wears sandals but when I last saw him he (wear) boots.
6 The house was in great disorder because he (redecorate) it.
7 The director didn't allow the actors to travel by air while they (work) on the film.
8 The car had nobody in it but the engine (run).
9 Two children (play) on the sand and two fishermen (lean) against an upturned boat.
10 I was alone in the house at that time because Mr Jones (work) in the garage and Mrs Jones (shop).
11 He said that he was the captain of a ship which (sail) that night for Marseilles.
12 Are you going to Rome? I thought that you (go) to Milan.
13 My wife and I (talk) about you the other day.
14 When I first met him he (study) painting.
15 There was a strong smell and the sound of frying. Obviously Mrs Jones (cook) fish.
16 Tom ate nothing for lunch because he (diet). He said that he (try) to lose 10 kilos.
17 Who you (talk) to on the telephone as I came in?
I (talk) to Mr Pitt.
18 As she (climb) the ladder it slipped sideways and she fell off it.
19 When I first met him he (work) in a restaurant.
20 He watched the children for a moment. Some of them (bathe) in the sea, others (look) for shells, others (play) in the sand.
21 Where he (live) when you saw him last?
22 She said that she couldn't come to the door because she (wash) her hair.
23 From the sounds it was clear that Mary (practise) the piano.
24 There had been an accident and men (carry) the injured people to an ambulance.
25 Two men (fight) at a street corner and a policeman (try) to stop them.
What they (fight) about?
Nobody seemed to know.
26 Tom (sit) in a corner with a book. I told him that he (read) in very bad light.
27 I went into the garden to see what the boys (do). James (weed) and Alexander (cut) the grass.
28 They had taken off the wheel of the car and (mend) the puncture. I asked when it would be ready.

29 When I arrived at the meeting the first speaker had just finished speaking and the audience (clap).
30 The traffic (make) so much noise that I couldn't hear what he (say).
31 While he (learn) to drive he had twenty-five accidents.
32 He had a bad fall while he (repair) his roof.
33 He was a little mad. He always (try) to prove that the earth was flat.
34 While we (fish) someone came to the house and left this note.
35 The exam had just begun and the candidates (write) their names at the top of their papers.
36 Just as I (wonder) what to do next, the phone rang.

12 The simple past and the past continuous

C PEG 172–8

Put the verbs in brackets into the simple past or the past continuous tense.

1 I lit the fire at 6.00 and it (burn) brightly when Tom came in at 7.00.
2 When I arrived the lecture had already started and the professor (write) on the overhead projector.
3 I (make) a cake when the light went out. I had to finish it in the dark.
4 I didn't want to meet Paul so when he entered the room I (leave).
5 Unfortunately when I arrived Ann just (leave), so we only had time for a few words.
6 He (have) a bath when the phone rang. Very unwillingly he (get) out of the bath and (go) to answer it.
7 He was very polite. Whenever his wife entered the room he (stand) up.
8 The admiral (play) bowls when he received news of the invasion. He (insist) on finishing the game.
9 My dog (walk) along quietly when Mr Pitt's Pekinese attacked him.
10 When I arrived she (have) lunch. She apologized for starting without me but said that she always (lunch) at 12.30.
11 He always (wear) a raincoat and (carry) an umbrella when he walked to the office.
12 Have you read his last book? Yes, I have.
What you (think) of it? I (like) it very much.
13 I (share) a flat with him when we were students. He always (complain) about my untidiness.
14 He suddenly (realize) that he (travel) in the wrong direction.

15 He (play) the guitar outside her house when someone opened the window and (throw) out a bucket of water.
16 I just (open) the letter when the wind (blow) it out of my hand.
17 The burglar (open) the safe when he (hear) footsteps. He immediately (put) out his torch and (crawl) under the bed.
18 When I (look) for my passport I (find) this old photograph.
19 You looked very busy when I saw you last night. What you (do)?
20 The boys (play) cards when they (hear) their father's step. They immediately (hide) the cards and (take) out their lesson books.
21 He (clean) his gun when it accidentally (go) off and (kill) him.
22 He (not allow) us to go out in the boat yesterday as a strong wind (blow).
23 As I (cross) the road I (step) on a banana skin and (fall) heavily.
24 I still (lie) on the road when I (see) a lorry approaching.
25 Luckily the driver (see) me and (stop) the lorry in time.
26 How you (damage) your car so badly?
I (run) into a lamp-post yesterday.
I suppose you (drive) too quickly or were not looking where you (go).
27 As he (get) into the bus it (start) suddenly and he (fall) backwards on to the road.
28 I (call) Paul at 7.00 but it wasn't necessary because he already (get) up.
29 When he (mend) the fuse he (get) a very bad shock.
30 When I (hear) his knock I (go) to the door and (open) it, but I (not recognize) him at first because I (not wear) my glasses.
31 When I came in they (sit) round the fire. Mr Pitt (do) a crossword puzzle, Mrs Pitt (knit), the others (read). Mrs Pitt (smile) at me and (say), 'Come and sit down.'
32 While the guests (dance) thieves (break) into the house and (steal) a lot of fur coats.
33 The next day, as they (know) that the police (look) for them, they (hide) the coats in a wood and (go) off in different directions.
34 She was very extravagant. She always (buy) herself new clothes.
35 Her mother often (tell) her that she (spend) too much money but she never (listen).
36 I looked over the wall and (see) Mr Pitt. He (plant) cabbages and (be) too busy to speak to me.

13 The simple past and the past continuous

B PEG 172–8

Put the verbs in brackets into the simple past or past continuous tense.

1 Mr Smith never (wake) up in time in the mornings and always (get) into trouble for being late; so one day he (go) to town and (buy) an alarm clock.

2 To get home he (have to) go through a field where a bad-tempered bull usually (graze).

3 This bull normally (not chase) people unless something (make) him angry. Unfortunately, as Mr Smith (cross) the field, his alarm clock (go) off.

4 This (annoy) the bull, who immediately (begin) to chase Mr Smith.

5 Mr Smith (carry) an open umbrella as it (rain) slightly. He (throw) the umbrella to the ground and (run) away as fast as he could.

6 The bull (stop) and (begin) to attack the umbrella. While he (do) this Mr Smith escaped.

7 When he (awake) she (sit) by the window. She (look) at something in the street, but when he (call) her she (turn) and (smile) at him.

8 Why you (interrupt) me just now? I (have) a very interesting conversation with Mr Pitt.

9 The murderer (carry) the corpse down the stairs when he (hear) a knock on the door.

10 When I (look) through your books I (notice) that you have a copy of *Murder in the Cathedral*.

11 As they (walk) along the road they (hear) a car coming from behind them. Tom (turn) round and (hold) up his hand. The car (stop).

12 When I (arrive) at the station Mary (wait) for me. She (wear) a blue dress and (look) very pretty. As soon as she (see) me she (wave) her umbrella and (shout) something, but I couldn't hear what she (say) because everybody (make) such a noise.

13 The prisoner (escape) by climbing the wall of the garden where he (work). He (wear) blue overalls and black shoes.

14 She said that the car (travel) at 40 k.p.h. when it (begin) to skid.

15 She said that she (not like) her present flat and (try) to find another.

16 While he (make) his speech the minister suddenly (feel) faint. But someone (bring) him a glass of water and after a few minutes he (be able) to continue.

17 When I (see) him he (paint) a portrait of his wife.
You (like) it?
He only just (start) when I (see) it, so I couldn't judge.

18 I (take) my friend to a murder trial the other day.
Who (be) tried?
A man called Bill Sykes.
Was he acquitted?
I don't know. They still (listen) to the evidence when we (leave).

19 I (be) sorry that I (have to) leave the party early, because I (enjoy) myself.

20 As we (come) here a policeman (stop) us. He (say) that he (look) for some stolen property and (ask) if he could search the car.

21 I (see) you yesterday from the bus. Why you (use) a stick?
I (use) a stick because I had hurt my leg that morning falling off a horse.
Whose horse you (ride)?

22 The floor was covered with balls of wool. Obviously Mrs Pitt (knit) something.

23 Ann said that she (be) on holiday. I (say) that I (hope) that she (enjoy) herself.

24 While he (water) the flowers it (begin) to rain. He (put) up his umbrella and (go) on watering.

25 I just (write) a cheque when I (remember) that I (have) nothing in the bank.

26 I (find) this ring as I (dig) in the garden. It looks very old. I wonder who it (belong) to?

27 When I last (see) her she (hurry) along the road to the station. I (ask) her where she (go) and she (say), 'London', but I don't think she (speak) the truth because there (not be) any train for London at that time.

28 The tailor said, 'Your suit will be ready on Monday.' But when I (call) on Monday he still (work) on it.

29 The teacher (come) into the classroom unusually early and one of the boys, who (smoke) a cigarette, (have) no time to put it out. So he (throw) it into his desk and (hope) for the best.

30 A little later the teacher (notice) that smoke (rise) from this desk. 'You (smoke) when I (come) in?' he (ask).

31 While I (swim) someone (steal) my clothes and I (have to) walk home in my swimsuit.

32 The men (say) that they (work) on the road outside my house and that they (want) some water to make tea.

33 He (say) that he (build) himself a house and that he (think) it would be ready in two years.

34 At 3 a.m. Mrs Pitt (wake) her husband and (say) that she (think) that someone (try) to get into the house.

35 Why you (lend) him that book? I still (read) it.
I'm sorry. I (not know) that you still (read) it.

36 I (come) in very late last night and unfortunately the dog (wake) up and (start) to bark. This (wake) my mother who (come) to the top of the stairs and (say), 'Who is there?'
I (say), 'It is me,' but she (not hear) me because the dog (bark) so loudly, so she (go) back to her room and (telephone) the police.

14 The present perfect tense

C PEG 179

Put the verbs in brackets into the present perfect tense, and fill the spaces by repeating the auxiliary.

e.g. You (wash) the plates? Yes, I . . .
Have you washed the plates. Yes, I have.

You (see) him lately? No, I . . .
Have you seen him lately? No, I haven't.

1 Where you (be)? I (be) to the dentist.
2 You (have) breakfast? Yes, I . . .
3 The post (come)? Yes, it . . .
4 You (see) my watch anywhere? No, I'm afraid I . . .
5 Someone (wind) the clock? Yes, Tom . . .
6 I (not finish) my letter yet.
7 He just (go) out.
8 Someone (take) my bicycle.
9 The phone (stop) ringing.
10 You (hear) from her lately? No, I . . .
11 I just (wash) that floor.
12 The cat (steal) the fish.
13 You (explain) the exercise? Yes, I . . .
14 There aren't any buses because the drivers (go) on strike.
15 You (have) enough to eat?
Yes, I (have) plenty, thank you.
16 Charles (pass) his exam? Yes, he . . .
17 How many bottles the milkman (leave)? He (leave) six.
18 I (live) here for ten years.
19 How long you (know) Mr Pitt? I (know) him for ten years.
20 Would you like some coffee? I just (make) some.
21 Mary (water) the tomatoes? Yes, I think she . . .

22 You (not make) a mistake? No, I'm sure I . . .
23 Why you (not mend) the fuse? I (not have) time.
24 You (dive) from the ten-metre board yet? No, I . . .
25 You ever (leave) a restaurant without paying the bill?
No, I . . .
26 I (ask) him to dinner several times.
27 He always (refuse).
28 You ever (ride) a camel?
29 I (buy) a new carpet. Come and look at it.
30 He (post) the letter?
31 Why he (not finish)? He (have) plenty of time.
32 I often (see) him but I never (speak) to him.
33 You ever (eat) caviar. No, I . . .
34 We just (hear) the most extraordinary news.
35 The police (recapture) the prisoners who escaped yesterday.
36 I (not pay) the telephone bill yet.

15 The present perfect and the simple past

C PEG 174, 180–4

a Fill the spaces by repeating the auxiliary used in the question, putting it into the negative where necessary.
b Put the verb in brackets into the present perfect or the simple past tense.

e.g. Have you seen that play? a Yes, I . . .
Yes, I have.
b Yes, I (be) there last night.
Yes, I was there last night.

1 Have you wound the clock?
a Yes, I . . .
b Yes, I (wind) it on Monday.

2 Have you ever eaten snails?
a No, I . . .
b Yes, I (eat) some at Tom's party last week.

3 Has she fed the dog?
a Yes, I think she . . .
b Yes, she (feed) him before lunch.

4 Have they repaired the road?
a No, they . . .
b They only (repair) part of it so far.

5 Have they done their homework?	a Yes, they (do) it all. b Yes, they (do) it before they left school.
6 Have you found the matches?	a No, I . . . b No, I (not find) them yet.
7 Have you made the coffee?	a Yes, I . . . b I (make) some yesterday: we can use that.
8 Have you been here before?	a No, I . . . b Yes, I (be) here several times.
9 Have you seen him lately?	a No, I . . . b No, I (not see) him since Christmas.
10 Have you been to the opera this week?	a Yes, I . . . b Yes, I (go) to *Faust* on Friday.
11 Have you ever driven this car?	a Yes, I (drive) it once or twice. b Yes, I (drive) it when you were away.
12 Has he missed his train?	a No, he . . . b Yes, he . . . . It (go) five minutes ago.
13 Have they been through Customs?	a Yes, they . . . b Yes, their luggage (be) examined at Victoria.
14 Has he spoken to her?	a Yes, he . . . b Yes, he (speak) to her on Friday.
15 Have you spent all your money?	a No, I only (spend) half of it. b Yes, I . . .
16 How much have you saved since Christmas?	a I (not save) anything. b I (save) £3.
17 Has his temperature gone down?	a No, it . . . b Yes, it (go) down last night.
18 Have you seen his garden?	a No, I (not see) it yet. b I (see) the house on Monday but I (not see) the garden.
19 Have you paid the bill?	a Yes, I . . . b Yes, I (pay) it while you were away.
20 Have you ever flown a plane?	a No, I . . . b Yes, I (fly) during the war.

21 Has your dog ever bitten anyone?	a Yes, he (bite) a policeman last week.
	b Yes, he (bite) me several times.
22 Have you planted your peas?	a Yes, I (plant) them on Tuesday.
	b No, I . . . yet.
23 Has he written to the paper?	a Yes, he . . .
	b Yes, he (write) at once.
24 Have you ever drunk pure alcohol?	a No, I . . .
	b I (drink) it once years ago and it nearly (kill) me.

16 The present perfect and the simple past

B PEG 174, 180–4

Put the verbs in brackets into the present perfect or the simple past tense. (In some sentences the present perfect continuous is also possible.)

1 This is my house.
How long you (live) here?
I (live) here since 1970.
2 He (live) in London for two years and then (go) to Edinburgh.
3 You (wear) your hair long when you were at school?
Yes, my mother (insist) on it.
4 But when I (leave) school I (cut) my hair and (wear) it short ever since.
5 Shakespeare (write) a lot of plays.
6 My brother (write) several plays. He just (finish) his second tragedy.
7 I (fly) over Loch Ness last week.
You (see) the Loch Ness monster?
8 I (not see) him for three years. I wonder where he is.
9 He (not smoke) for two weeks. He is trying to give it up.
10 Chopin (compose) some of his music in Majorca.
11 When he (arrive)? He (arrive) at 2.00.
12 You (lock) the door before you left the house?
13 I (read) his books when I was at school. I (enjoy) them very much.
14 I can't go out because I (not finish) my work.
15 I never (drink) whisky. Well, have some now.

16 I (write) the letter but I can't find a stamp.
17 The clock is slow. It isn't slow, it (stop).
18 Here are your shoes; I just (clean) them.
19 I (leave) home at 8.00 and (get) here at twelve.
20 I (do) this sort of work when I (be) in the army.
21 He just (go) out.
22 He (go) out ten minutes ago.
23 You (have) breakfast yet? Yes, I (have) it at 8.00.
24 I (meet) him last June.
25 You (see) the moon last night?
26 The concert (begin) at 2.30 and (last) for two hours. Everyone (enjoy) it very much.
27 The play just (begin). You are a little late.
28 The newspaper (come)? Yes, Ann is reading it.
29 The actors (arrive) yesterday and (start) rehearsals early this morning.
30 It (be) very cold this year. I wonder when it is going to get warmer.
31 Cervantes (write) *Don Quixote*.
32 We (miss) the bus. Now we'll have to walk.
33 He (break) his leg in a skiing accident last year.
34 Mr Pound is the bank manager. He (be) here for five years.
35 Mr Count (work) as a cashier for twenty-five years. Then he (retire) and (go) to live in the country.
36 You (be) here before?
Yes, I (spend) my holidays here last year.
You (have) a good time?
No, it never (stop) raining.

17 The present perfect and the simple past

A PEG 174, 180–4

Put the verbs in brackets into the present perfect or simple past tense. Fill the spaces by repeating the auxiliary used in the preceding verb.

e.g. You (see) Mary on Monday: Yes, I . . .
Did you see Mary on Monday? Yes, I did.

1 Where is Tom?
I (not see) him today, but he (tell) Mary that he'd be in for dinner.
2 I (buy) this in Bond Street.
How much you (pay) for it?
I (pay) £100.

3 Where you (find) this knife?
I (find) it in the garden.
Why you (not leave) it there?
4 I (lose) my black gloves. You (see) them anywhere?
No, I'm afraid I . . . When you last (wear) them?
I (wear) them at the theatre last night.
Perhaps you (leave) them at the theatre.
5 Do you know that lady who just (leave) the shop?
Yes, that is Miss Thrift. Is she a customer of yours?
Not exactly. She (be) in here several times but she never (buy) anything.
6 He (leave) the house at 8.00.
Where he (go)?
I (not see) where he (go).
7 He (serve) in the First World War.
When that war (begin)?
It (begin) in 1914 and (last) for four years.
8 Who you (vote) for at the last election?
I (vote) for Mr Pitt.
He (not be) elected, (be) he?
No, he (lose) his deposit.
9 You (like) your last job?
I (like) it at first but then I (quarrel) with my employer and he (dismiss) me.
How long you (be) there?
I (be) there for two weeks.
10 I (not know) that you (know) Mrs Pitt. How long you (know) her?
I (know) her for ten years.
11 That is Mr Minus, who teaches me mathematics, but he (not have) time to teach me much. I only (be) in his class for a week.
12 You (hear) his speech on the radio last night?
Yes, I . . .
What you (think) of it?
13 I (not know) that you (be) here. You (be) here long?
Yes, I (be) here two months.
You (be) to the Cathedral?
Yes, I (go) there last Sunday.
14 You ever (try) to give up smoking?
Yes, I (try) last year, but then I (find) that I was getting fat so I (start) again.
15 You (see) today's paper?
No, anything interesting (happen)?

Yes, several of the patients (escape) from our local mental hospital.

16 Mary (feed) the cat?
Yes, she (feed) him before lunch.
What she (give) him?
She (give) him some fish.

17 How long you (know) your new assistant?
I (know) him for two years.
What he (do) before he (come) here?
I think he (be) in prison.

18 I (not see) your aunt recently.
No. She (not be) out of her house since she (buy) her colour TV.

19 The plumber (be) here yet?
Yes, but he only (stay) for an hour.
What he (do) in that time?
He (turn) off the water and (empty) the tank.

20 Where you (be)?
I (be) out in a yacht.
You (enjoy) it?
Yes, very much. We (take) part in a race.
You (win)?
No, we (come) in last.

21 How long that horrible monument (be) there?
It (be) there six months. Lots of people (write) to the Town Council asking them to take it away but so far nothing (be) done.

22 I just (be) to the film *War and Peace*. You (see) it?
No, I . . . Is it like the book?
I (not read) the book.
I (read) it when I (be) at school.
When Tolstoy (write) it?
He (write) it in 1868.
He (write) anything else?

23 Hannibal (bring) elephants across the Alps.
Why he (do) that?
He (want) to use them in battle.

24 Where you (be)? I (be) to the dentist.
He (take) out your bad tooth? Yes, he . . .
It (hurt)? Yes, horribly.

25 She (say) that she'd phone me this morning, but it is now 12.30 and she (not phone) yet.

26 I just (receive) a letter saying that we (not pay) this quarter's electricity bill. I (not give) you the money for that last week?
Yes, you . . . but I'm afraid I (spend) it on something else.

27 How long you (be) out of work?
I'm not out of work now. I just (start) a new job.
How you (find) the job?
I (answer) an advertisement in the paper.
28 You (finish) checking the accounts?
No, not quite. I (do) about half so far.
29 I (cut) my hand rather badly. Have you a bandage?
I'll get you one. How it (happen)?
I was chopping some wood and the axe (slip).
30 How you (get) that scar?
I (get) it in a car accident a year ago.
31 You (meet) my brother at the lecture yesterday?
Yes, I . . . We (have) coffee together afterwards.
32 He (lose) his job last month and since then he (be) out of work.
Why he (lose) his job?
He (be) very rude to Mr Pitt.
33 What are all those people looking at?
There (be) an accident.
You (see) what (happen)?
Yes, a motor cycle (run) into a lorry.
34 I (phone) you twice yesterday and (get) no answer.
35 Originally horses used in bull fights (not wear) any protection, but for some time now they (wear) special padding.

18 The present perfect continuous tense

C PEG 185–6

Put the verbs in brackets into the present perfect continuous tense.

1 I (make) cakes. That is why my hands are all covered with flour.
2 Her phone (ring) for ten minutes. I wonder why she doesn't answer it.
3 He (overwork). That is why he looks so tired.
4 There is sawdust in your hair.
I'm not surprised. I (cut) down a tree.
5 Have you seen my bag anywhere? I (look) for it for ages.
6 What you (do)? I (work) in the laboratory.
7 He (study) Russian for two years and doesn't even know the alphabet yet.
8 How long you (wait) for me? I (wait) about half an hour.
9 It (rain) for two days now. There'll be a flood soon.

10 We (argue) about this for two hours now. Perhaps we should stop!
11 I (bathe). That's why my hair is all wet.
12 You (drive) all day. Let me drive now.
13 How long you (wear) glasses?
14 The petrol gauge (say) 'Empty' for quite a long time now. Don't you think we should get some petrol?
15 I'm sorry for keeping you waiting. I (try) to make a telephone call to Rome.
16 You (not eat) enough lately. That's why you feel irritable.
17 He (speak) for an hour now. I expect he'll soon be finished.
18 That aeroplane (fly) round the house for the last hour; do you think the pilot wants to drop a bomb on us?
19 The radio (play) since 7 a.m. I wish someone would turn it off.
20 I (shop) all day and I haven't a penny left.
21 We (live) here since 1977.
22 I'm on a diet. I (eat) nothing but bananas for the last month.
23 The children (look) forward to this holiday for months.
24 That pipe (leak) for ages. We must get it mended.
25 Tom (dig) in the garden all afternoon. Why you not (help) him?
26 I (ask) you to mend that window for six weeks. When are you going to do it?
27 Someone (use) my bicycle. The chain's fallen off.
28 How long you (drive)? I (drive) for ten years.
29 The trial (go) on for a long time. I wonder what the verdict will be.
30 It (snow) for three days now. The roads will be blocked if it doesn't stop soon.
31 Mary (cry)?
No, she (not cry), she (peel) onions.
32 The car (make) a very curious noise ever since it ran out of oil.
33 He walked very unsteadily up the stairs and his wife said, 'You (drink)!'
34 Your fingers are very brown. You (smoke) too much.
35 You usually know when someone (eat) garlic.
36 Ever since he came to us that man (try) to make trouble.

19 The present perfect and the present perfect continuous

B PEG 187–8

Put the verbs in brackets into the present perfect or the present perfect continuous tense. (In some cases either could be used.)

1 We (walk) ten kilometres.
2 We (walk) for three hours.
3 You (walk) too fast. That's why you are tired.
4 I (make) sausage rolls for the party all the morning.
5 How many you (make)? I (make) 200.
6 That boy (eat) seven ice-creams.
7 He (not stop) eating since he arrived.
8 The driver (drink). I think someone else ought to drive.
9 I (pull) up 100 dandelions.
10 I (pull) up dandelions all day.
11 What you (do)? We (pick) apples.
12 How many you (pick)? We (pick) ten baskets.
13 I (sleep) on every bed in this house and I don't like any of them.
14 He (sleep) since ten o'clock. It's time he woke up.
15 He (ride); that's why he is wearing breeches.
16 I (ride) all the horses in this stable.
17 What a lovely smell! Mary (make) jam.
18 The students (work) very well this term.
19 I only (hear) from him twice since he went away.
20 I (hear) from her regularly. She is a very good correspondent.
21 I (grease) my car. That's why my hands are so dirty.
22 I (polish) this table all the morning and Mrs Pitt isn't satisfied with it yet.
23 I (work) for him for ten years and he never once (say) 'Good morning' to me.
24 He (teach) in this school for five years.
25 I (teach) hundreds of students but I never (meet) such a hopeless class as this.
26 Why you (be) so long in the garage?
The tyres were flat; I (pump) them up.
27 I (pump) up three tyres. Would you like to do the fourth?
28 I (look) for mushrooms but I (not find) any.
29 He (cough) a lot lately. He ought to give up smoking.
30 You (hear) the news? Tom and Ann are engaged!
That's not new, I (know) it for ages!

31 I (try) to finish this letter for the last half-hour. I wish you'd go away or stop talking.
I hardly (say) anything.
32 The driver of that car (sound) his horn for the last ten minutes.
33 It (rain) for two hours and the ground is too wet to play on, so the match (be) postponed.
34 He (hope) for a rise in salary for six months but he (not dare) to ask for it yet.
35 Mr Smith, you (whisper) to the student on your right for the last five minutes. You (help) him with his exam paper or he (help) you?
36 Why you (make) such a horrible noise?
I (lose) my key and I (try) to wake my wife by throwing stones at her window.
You (throw) stones at the wrong window. You live next door.

20 *for* and *since*

C PEG 82, 183

Fill the spaces in the following sentences by using **for** or **since**.

1 We've been fishing . . . two hours.
2 I've been working in this office . . . a month.
3 They've been living in France . . . 1970.
4 He has been in prison . . . a year.
5 I've known that . . . a long time.
6 That man has been standing there . . . six o'clock.
7 She has worn the same hat . . . 1975.
8 Things have changed . . . I was a girl.
9 The kettle has been boiling . . . a quarter of an hour.
10 The central heating has been on . . . October.
11 That trunk has been in the hall . . . a year.
12 He has been very ill . . . the last month.
13 I've been using this machine . . . twelve years.
14 We've been waiting . . . half an hour.
15 Mr Pitt has been in hospital . . . his accident.
16 He hasn't spoken to me . . . the last committee meeting.
17 I have been very patient with you . . . several years.
18 They have been on strike . . . November.
19 The strike has lasted . . . six months.
20 It has been very foggy . . . early morning.

21 They have been quarrelling ever . . . they got married.
22 I've been awake . . . four o'clock.
23 I've been awake . . . a long time.
24 We've had no gas . . . the strike began.
25 I've earned my own living . . . I left school.
26 Nobody has seen him . . . last week.
27 The police have been looking for me . . . four days.
28 I haven't worn low-heeled shoes . . . I was at school.
29 He had a bad fall last week and . . . then he hasn't left the house.
30 He has been under water . . . half an hour.
31 That tree has been there . . . 2,000 years.
32 He has been Minister of Education . . . 1976.
33 I've been trying to open this door . . . forty-five minutes.
34 He hasn't eaten anything . . . twenty-four hours.
35 We've had terrible weather . . . the last month.
36 Nobody has come to see us . . . we bought these bloodhounds.

2 Future and conditional tenses

21 The present continuous tense

C PEG 197

Put the verbs in brackets into the present continuous tense.

1 They are going to drill for oil here. They (start) on Monday.
2 My uncle (make) a speech on Friday.
3 I (take) my sister to the ballet tomorrow.
4 She (call) for me at six.
5 He (play) at Wimbledon next summer.
6 I (meet) her at the station at ten.
7 The sales (start) on Monday.
8 How you (get) to the party tomorrow?
I (go) by car.
Who (drive)?
9 The piano tuner (come) this afternoon.
10 You (give) up anything for Lent?
Yes, I (give) up cigarettes.
11 The windows (be) cleaned this afternoon. Then we'll be able to see out.
12 She (come) out of hospital next week.
13 We (have) dinner early tonight as we (go) to the theatre.
14 Where you (go) for your holidays this year?
I (go) to Holland.
15 He (give) a lecture tonight.
16 I (have) my photograph taken tomorrow.
17 I (buy) her a burglar alarm for a wedding present.
18 The elections (be) held next week.
19 I (have) lunch with my aunt on Thursday.
20 The committee (meet) next Wednesday.
21 My grandparents (celebrate) their golden wedding next week.
22 I (lend) him my car for his holidays.
23 The strikers (return) to work next week.
24 Smith's (open) a new branch in this street in July.
25 We've bought a new house and (move) in very soon.

26 I (take) up judo next winter.
27 They (get) married next week.
28 You (do) anything tonight?
Yes, I (go) to my carpentry class.
29 The Prime Minister (fly) to America tomorrow.
30 He (start) a new job on Friday.
31 The Queen (give) a garden party next week. You (go)?
32 My brother (be) released on Tuesday. I (meet) him outside the prison.
33 I (catch) the 6.30 plane tomorrow.
Where you (leave) your car?
I (leave) it at the airport.
34 Her mother (send) her to France next year.
35 I (go) to the dentist tomorrow. Miss Pitt (take) my class.
36 I (let) my flat to my American cousins next year.

22 The *be going to* form

C PEG 198–200

Put the verbs in brackets into the **be going to** form.

1 You (miss) your train.
2 The pressure cooker (explode).
3 When your husband (cut) the grass?
4 She (dye) the old curtains blue.
5 We (make) this whisky bottle into a lamp.
6 What you (do) with this room?
I (paint) the walls in black and white stripes.
7 The umpire (blow) his whistle.
8 You (eat) all that?
9 That man with the tomato in his hand (throw) it at the speaker.
10 That door (slam).
11 The bull (attack) us.
12 It (rain). Look at those clouds.
13 The cat (have) kittens.
14 The men in the helicopter (try) to rescue the man in the water.
15 That rider (fall) off.
16 These swans (eat) all our sandwiches.
17 The Lord Mayor is standing up. He (make) a speech.
18 He (grow) a beard when he leaves school.
19 This aeroplane (crash).

20 I (stop) here for a moment to get some petrol.
21 You (ask) him to help you?
22 I've lent you my car once. I (not do) it again.
23 I have seen the play. Now I (read) the book.
24 My son (be) a frogman when he grows up.
25 I (not sleep) in this room. It is haunted.
26 We (buy) a metal detector and look for buried treasure.
27 You (reserve) a seat?
28 I (plant) an oak tree here.
29 The dog (bury) the bone.
30 I (have) a bath.
31 I (smuggle) this out of the country.
32 There was very little blossom this spring. Apples (be) scarce.
33 I don't like this macaroni. I (not finish) it.
34 I (not stay) here another minute.
35 They (try) him for manslaughter when he comes out of hospital.
36 We (make) a lot of money out of this.

23 The present continuous and the *be going to* form

C PEG 197–200

Planned future actions can be expressed by the present continuous tense with a time expression or by the **be going to** form with or without a time expression. The present continuous is mainly used for very definite arrangements in the near future. The **be going to** form can be used more widely.

Use the present continuous where possible in the following sentences and put the remaining verbs into the **be going to** form.

1 I (play) bridge tonight with Tom and Ann.
2 He (have) an operation next week.
3 It's very cold. I (light) a fire.
4 We (have) some friends to lunch tomorrow.
5 I've bought a piano; it (be) delivered this afternoon.
Where you (put) it?
I (put) it in the dining room.
6 You (go) to the auction tomorrow?
Yes, I (go) but I (not buy) anything.
7 I've reminded you once; I (not do) it again.
8 I (have) my hair cut this afternoon.

9 My nephew (come) to stay with me next weekend.
Where you (put) him?
I (put) him in the room in the tower.
10 Our class (start) German next term.
11 I (spend) a few days in London next week.
12 The Town Council (build) a new school here.
13 What you (tell) the police? I (tell) them the truth.
14 He (start) tomorrow.
15 The Queen (open) Parliament next month.
16 The Prime Minister (speak) on TV tonight.
17 This shop (close) down next week.
18 When you (have) your next lesson?
I (have) it on Monday.
19 I (collect) my new dress this afternoon.
20 We (take) the children to the seaside this summer.
21 I (give) him a football for his next birthday.
22 She (sing) in her first big concert next month.
23 He (go) to Spain for his holidays.
He (fly)?
No, he (go) by boat.
24 She (see) a specialist next week.
25 He (wash) the car?
26 He (ring) me up tonight.
27 The inspector (ask) you a few questions.
28 Her parents (give) a party for her next month. They (invite) sixty guests.
29 Have you got a ticket for the big match on Saturday?
No, I don't even know who (play).
France (play) England.
30 They (launch) a ship this afternoon. You (come) to see it?
31 What you (do) with the money?
32 I (pick) you up at 6.30; don't forget.
33 Where you (go) tonight?
I (go) out with Peter. He (call) for me at eight.
34 I (compete) in the bicycle race tomorrow.
35 Mr Pitt has just phoned to say that he (not come) back till Wednesday night.
36 I (read) you his answer to my letter of complaint.

24 The future tense

C PEG 201–2

Put the verbs in brackets into the future tense.

1 I (know) the result in a week.
2 You (be) in Rome tonight.
3 You (have) time to help me tomorrow?
4 It (matter) if I don't come home till morning?
5 You (be) able to drive after another five lessons.
6 Do you think that he (recognize) me?
7 Unless he runs he (not catch) the train.
8 He (lend) it to you if you ask him.
9 I hope I (find) it.
10 If petrol pump attendants go on strike we (not have) any petrol.
11 He (believe) whatever you tell him.
12 I (remember) this day all my life.
13 Perhaps he (arrive) in time for lunch.
14 If he works well I (pay) him £10.
15 I wonder how many of us still (be) here next year.
16 If you think it over you (see) that I am right.
17 If you learn another language you (get) a better job.
18 I am sure that you (like) our new house.
19 Newspaper announcement: The President (drive) along the High Street in an open carriage.
20 He (mind) if I bring my dog?
21 You (need) a visa if you are going to Spain.
22 If you open that trapdoor you (see) some steps.
23 You (feel) better when you've had a meal.
24 He (be) offended if you don't invite him.
25 She (have) £400 a year when she is twenty-one.
26 If you put any more polish on that floor someone (slip) on it.
27 I wonder if he (succeed).
28 Papers (not be) delivered on the Bank Holiday.
29 I hope he (remember) to buy wine.
30 If you leave your skateboard on the path someone (fall) over it.
31 If they fall over it and hurt themselves they (sue) you.
32 Announcement: Mrs Pitt (present) the prizes.
33 If you want twenty cigarettes you (have) to give me more money.
34 Notice: The management (not be) responsible for articles left on the seats.

35 If I drop this it (explode).
36 What your father (say) when he hears about this accident?
He (not say) much but he (not lend) me the car again.

25 The present continuous and the future tense

C PEG 197, 203

Put the verbs in brackets into the present continuous or the future tense, using the present continuous where possible.

(The **be going to** form could be used here instead of the present continuous, but for the sake of simplicity students are advised to use only the two tenses first mentioned.)

1 I am sure that I (recognize) him.
2 I (see) her tomorrow.
3 He (play) in a tennis match on Friday.
4 She (come) back on Monday.
5 I (go) again next year.
6 We (know) tonight.
7 You pay and I (owe) you the money.
8 I (believe) it when I see it.
9 I (have) my car repainted next week.
10 I hope that you (have) a good time tomorrow.
11 His speech (be) broadcast tonight.
12 The sweep (come) at eight tomorrow.
13 Tom (catch) the 7.40 train.
14 Where you (meet) them?
I (meet) them at midnight in the middle of the wood.
15 What horse you (ride) tomorrow?
16 Look! I've broken the teapot. What Mrs Pitt (say)?
She (not mind); she never liked that one.
17 I've left the light on. It (matter)?
18 He (not forget) to come.
19 He (leave) in a few days.
20 I (remember) it.
21 If you drop that bottle it (break).
22 I never (forgive) him.
23 I'm sure that you (like) him.
24 They (lay) the foundations next week.
25 You (see) a signpost at the end of the road.

26 He has cut my hair too short.
Don't worry; it (grow) again very quickly.
27 You (understand) when you are older.
28 The cat (scratch) you if you pull its tail.
29 I (be) back at 8.30.
30 If he doesn't work hard he (not pass) his exam.
31 She (go) on a cruise next summer.
32 I (move) to a new flat next week.
33 I am sorry that the child saw the accident.
I don't think it matters. He soon (forget) all about it.
34 I (wait) here till he comes back.
35 He (not write) to you unless you write to him.
36 There (be) a big meeting here tomorrow.

26 *will* + infinitive and the *be going to* form

B PEG 199

Future with intention can usually be expressed by **will** + infinitive or the **be going to** form. Very often either of these can be used, but when the intention is clearly premeditated the **be going to** form must be used, and when the intention is clearly unpremeditated we must use **will** + infinitive.

Put the verbs in brackets into one of these two forms. (In some of the examples the present continuous could be used instead of the **be going to** form.)

1 The fire has gone out!
So it has. I (go) and get some sticks.
2 Did you remember to book seats?
Oh no, I forgot. I (telephone) for them now.
3 He has just been taken to hospital with a broken leg.
I'm sorry to hear that. I (send) him some grapes.
4 I've hired a typewriter and I (learn) to type.
5 I see that you are wearing your gardening gloves. You (do) some weeding?
6 I can't understand this letter.
I (call) my son. He (translate) it for you.
7 You (buy) bread?
No, because I (not eat) it any more. I (eat) biscuits instead.
8 A lot of paint was delivered here today. You (redecorate) your kitchen?

9 Why are you getting out the jack?
We have a puncture and I (change) the wheel.
I (help) you.
10 Look what I've just bought at an auction!
What an extraordinary thing! Where you (put) it?
11 Why are you peeling that bit of garlic?
I (put) it in the stew.
12 What you (do) when you grow up?
I (be) an acrobat in a circus.
13 Why are you taking out all your dresses?
I (shorten) the skirts.
14 Will you lend me your season ticket?
No, I (not lend) it to you. It is against the law.
15 That tree makes the house very dark.
Very well, I (cut) it down.
16 I've just enrolled at the local technical college. I (attend) pottery classes next winter.
17 How do I get from here to London Bridge?
I don't know, but I (ask) that policeman.
18 Why are you carrying a corkscrew?
I (open) a bottle of wine.
19 I see that you've got a letter from Charles. What does he say?
I don't know. I (not read) the letter now as I haven't time.
20 My brother has just returned from America.
Oh good, we (ask) him to our next party.
21 Why have you set your alarm to go off at five-thirty?
Because I (get) up then. I've got a lot to do.
22 I hear that you've decided to go on a diet. When you (start)?
I (start) on Monday.
23 You look frozen. Sit down by the fire and I (make) you a cup of tea.
24 They've brought a rope and they (tow) the car to a garage.
25 I haven't bought any cigarettes because I (give) up smoking.
26 I have tried to explain but she doesn't understand English.
I (say) it to her in Finnish: perhaps she'll understand that.
27 I've come out without any money.
Never mind, I (lend) you some. How much do you want?
28 Do you see that car? They (raffle) it for charity.
29 Why are you taking up that floor board?
I (put) my money under the floor. I don't trust banks.
30 Child: I've torn my dress.
Mother: I (mend) it for you.
31 I'm catching the 6.30 train.

So am I. I (give) you a lift to the station.
32 I've bought some blue velvet and I (make) curtains for the drawing room.
33 Why are you carrying that saw?
I (shorten) the legs of the dining room table.
34 You won't need the big basket, will you?
Oh yes, I will, I (buy) a lot of vegetables.
35 I've planned my future for the next ten years.
That is very clever of you. What you (do) when you leave the university?
36 Why are you putting that old loaf into a paper bag?
I (give) it to Mrs Pitt for her hens.

27 *will* + infinitive and the *be going to* form

B PEG 199

Both **will you** and **are you going to** can introduce questions about future intentions. But **will you** very often introduces a request or invitation. For this reason **are you going to** is more usual than **will you** in questions about intentions. **are you going to** must of course be used when the intention is obviously premeditated. (See also Exercise 31.)

Put the verbs in brackets into one of these two forms. Where both are possible it will be noted in the key. (In some examples the present continuous tense could be used instead of the **be going to** form.) The exercise contains requests, invitations, and questions about intentions.

1 You (open) the door for me, please? Yes, certainly.
2 You (do) the washing-up tonight?
No, I think it can wait till tomorrow.
3 I'm looking for my easel.
You (paint) someone's portrait?
4 You (read) aloud to me while I do the ironing?
With pleasure. What book would you like?
5 You (eat) any more of this, or shall I tell the waiter to take it away?
6 You aren't wearing your climbing boots. You (not climb) the mountain?
7 I'm going to the football match. You (come) with me?
Thank you very much. I'd love to.
8 You (put) my car away for me, please? Yes, certainly.

9 You (have) another cup of coffee? No, thank you.
10 Why did you buy all these eggs? You (make) an enormous omelette?
11 There's the phone again. Lift the receiver off its rest and put it down again, will you?
You (not answer) it?
12 You (come) and see me after the class? I want to discuss your work with you.
13 I see that you have ordered the *Guardian*. You really (read) it?
14 You (buy) stamps?
Yes, I am.
Then you (buy) some for me, please?
15 You (lend) me your fishing rod?
Yes, of course. Where you (fish)?
16 You (finish) this book or shall I take it back to the library?
17 You (give) me 10p, please?
Yes, here you are. You (make) a telephone call?
18 You (leave) that coil of barbed wire in the hall? Someone will fall over it if you do.
19 You (bath) your dog? Yes, you (help) me?
20 You (drive), please? I don't like driving at night.
21 You (ride) that horse? He looks very bad-tempered to me.
22 You (eat) it raw? You will be ill if you do.
23 You (have) some of this cake? I made it myself.
24 You really (call) the fire brigade? I don't think it is at all necessary.
25 You (paint) the whole room by yourself? It will take you ages.
26 You (be) ready in five minutes?
27 Hostess: You (sit) here, please, beside Mr Pitt?
28 You (do) something for me?
Yes, of course, what is it?
29 You (be) angry if he refuses to help you?
30 Why have you brought your typewriter? You (work) this weekend?
31 You (call) me at six? I have to catch an early train.
32 You (walk) there in this rain? You'll get awfully wet.
33 You (sign) here, please?
34 What are all these notes for? You (give) a lecture?
35 Why do you want a candle? You (explore) the caves?
36 If I catch the fish, you (cook) them for me?

28 The future continuous tense
C PEG 205

This tense can be used

1 with a point in time to indicate that the action will begin before this time and continue after it.

2 with or without a time to express a future without intention. In this way it is very like the present continuous, but it is not, like the present continuous, restricted in time and is a more detached and casual way of expressing the future. It often implies that the action will occur in the ordinary course of events or as a matter of routine.

(Except when used as in 1, above, this tense can usually be replaced by one of the other future forms, though the exact shade of meaning may then be lost.)

Put the verbs in brackets into the future continuous tense.

1 This time next month I (sit) on a beach.
2 When you arrive I probably (pick) fruit.
3 When we reach England it very likely (rain).
4 In a few days time we (fly) over the Pyrenees.
5 I'll call for her at eight.
No, don't; she still (have) breakfast then.
6 I (wait) for you when you come out.
7 When you next see me I (wear) my new dress.
8 My son will be in the sixth form next year.
That means that old Dr Adder (teach) him mathematics.
9 I'll give Jack your message. I can do it easily because I (see) him tomorrow. We go to work on the same train.
10 You (do) geometry next term.
11 I'll look out for you at the parade.
Do, but I (wear) uniform so you may find it hard to recognize me.
12 We have to do night duty here. I (do) mine next week.
13 In a hundred years' time people (go) to Mars for their holidays.
14 I (use) the car this afternoon.
15 I (see) you again.
16 It's a serious injury but he (walk) again in six weeks.
17 I'll come at three o'clock.
Good, I (expect) you.
18 They are pulling down all the old houses in this street. I expect they (pull) down mine in a few years' time.

19 I'd like to see your new flat.
Well, come tomorrow, but it (not look) its best, for the painters still (work) on it.
20 Stand there, they (change) the guard in a minute and you'll get a good view.
21 You'd better go back now, your mother (wonder) where you are.
22 In fifty years' time we (live) entirely on pills.
23 What do you think the children (do) when we get home?
I expect they (have) their supper.
24 The garden (look) its best next month.
25 It won't be easy to get out of the country. The police (watch) all the ports.
26 What the tide (do) at six tomorrow morning?
It (come) in.
27 I've just remembered that I left the bathroom taps on. I expect the water (flow) down the stairs by now.
28 You (need) your camera tomorrow or can I borrow it?
29 We've just got to the top in time. The sun (rise) in a minute.
30 Air hostess: We (take off) in a few minutes. Please fasten your safety belts.
31 We'd better go out tomorrow because Mary (practise) the piano all day.
32 Don't ring her up now, she (put) the children to bed. Ring later.
33 We are making a house-to-house collection of things for the jumble sale. We (come) to your house next week.
34 That football club has lost some of its players. They (look out) for new men.
35 When I get home my dog (sit) at the door waiting for me.
36 Let's go down to the harbour; the fishing boats all (come) in because of the gale.

29 *will* + infinitive and the future continuous

B PEG 205, 208

See note for previous exercise.

Put the verbs in brackets into the appropriate future form, using **will** + infinitive or the future continuous. (Where alternative forms are possible they will be given in the key.)

1 There is going to be a bus strike. Everyone (walk) to work next week.

2 You've just missed the last train! Never mind, I (walk).
3 I'll ring you tomorrow at six.
No, don't ring at six; I (bath) the baby then. Ring later.
4 Mother: Your face is dirty.
Child: All right, I (wash) it.
5 Will you have lunch with me on the 24th?
I'd love to, but I'm afraid I (do) my exam then.
6 I (work) for Mr Pitt next week as his own secretary will be away.
7 The headmaster said: 'Smith and Brown (report) to me at six o'clock.' Smith and Brown looked horrified.
8 Why did you take his razor? He (look) for it everywhere tomorrow.
9 I hope you'll do well in the race tomorrow. I (think) of you.
10 Notice on board ship: In the event of an emergency all passengers (assemble) on the boat deck.
11 I don't feel well enough to go to the station to meet him.
I (meet) him for you. Tell me how I'll recognize him.
He (wear) a black and white school cap.
12 I (leave) these flowers at the hospital for you. I (go) there anyway to visit my cousin.
13 You ought to try to get a ticket for the Spectators' Gallery next week; they (debate) international fishing rights.
14 You've left the light on.
Oh, so I have. I (go) and turn it off.
15 I've just been appointed assistant at the local library.
Then you (work) under my sister. She is head librarian there.
16 I want to post this letter but I don't want to go out in the rain.
I (post) it for you. I (go) out anyway as I have to take the dog for a walk.
17 The prima ballerina is ill so I expect her understudy (dance) instead.
18 Today is Guy Fawkes' Day; this evening people (let) off fireworks and (make) bonfires in the streets.
19 Military order: Sentries (remain) on duty till they are relieved.
20 This time next Monday I (sit) in a Paris café reading *Le Figaro*.
You (not read). You'll be looking at all the pretty girls.
21 Wages have gone up, so I suppose prices (go up) too.
22 It is nearly autumn; soon the leaves (change) colour.
23 Mother (on phone): My son has just burnt his hand very badly.
Doctor: I (come) at once.
24 Customer in restaurant: Waiter, this plate is dirty.
Waiter: I'm sorry, sir, I (bring) you another.
25 In a few years' time we all (live) in houses heated by solar energy.
26 It's beginning to get dark; the street lights (go on) in a few minutes.

27 We (not play) poker at the party tonight; our hostess doesn't approve of cards.
28 Let's wait here; the swing bridge (open) in a minute to let that ship through.
29 Guest: May I use your phone to ring for a taxi?
Hostess: Oh, there's no need for that; my son (drive) you home.
30 Come on deck; we (enter) harbour in a few minutes.
31 Before you leave the office you (hand) the keys of the safe to Mr Pitt. Do you understand?
Yes, sir.
32 Are you nearly ready? Our guests (arrive) any minute.
33 Loudspeaker announcement: The ship (leave) in a few minutes and all persons not travelling are asked to go ashore.
34 Now that the parking regulations have become stricter, more people (use) public transport and (leave) their cars at home.
35 I've got rats in my basement and I don't know how to get rid of them.
I (bring) my dog round whenever you like. He (catch) them for you.
36 I'm afraid I've just broken your goldfish bowl.
Never mind, I (put) the goldfish in the bath.

30 *won't* + infinitive and the future continuous negative

B PEG 208

won't + infinitive (except when used as part of the ordinary future tense, **shall/will**) usually implies that the subject refuses to perform a certain action. The negative future continuous tense merely states that a certain action will not take place.

Put the verbs in brackets into the appropriate future form, using **won't** + infinitive or the future continuous negative. (Where other future forms are also possible this will be noted in the key.)

1 I don't like that man and I (not help) him.
2 He (not meet) her, because they will be in different places.
3 The gardener (not cut) down the tree. He says that it is perfectly all right as it is.
4 The gardener (not cut) the grass for some time, because I've got a lot of other jobs for him to do first.
5 Tom (not come) to our party, because he will be away on that date.
6 Peter says that he (not come) to our party. He doesn't approve of parties.

7 She says that she (not lend) me the book, because I never give books back.
8 Mr Pitt (not speak) at the meeting tonight, because he has unexpectedly had to go to hospital.
9 I'll work under anyone except my brother. I (not work) under him.
10 We'll be in the same firm, but we (not work) together, because we'll be in different departments.
11 I (not have) that pupil in my class. She is far too noisy.
12 I (not teach) you next week, as I have to go to Paris.
13 He is so angry with his sister that he (not speak) to her.
14 I'll give your message to my sister when I write; but I (not write) for some time, as I only write once a month and I posted a letter to her yesterday.
15 I (not feed) your dog again. He always tries to bite me when I come near him.
16 They were very rude to me. I (not go) there again.
17 He said. 'I (not paint) you in that dress. It does not suit you.'
18 I (not take) any photographs for some time because my camera is being repaired.
19 I (not borrow) his van again. The brakes don't work properly.
20 That boy (not wash) his face. He likes being dirty.
21 You can have the car tomorrow if you like. I (not use) it as I'll be far too busy to go out.
22 She says that she (not send) the child to school, no matter what we say. She thinks it is far better to educate children at home.
23 He says he (not play) for them again, because they aren't giving him enough money.
24 She (not sing) at the next concert, because she has had to go home suddenly.
25 I (not play) cards with you again. You always cheat.
26 She (not take) part in the bridge tournament, because she'll be away then.
27 I (not eat) any more of this; I feel queer already.
28 I (not eat) curry again for a long time, because I am going to stay in a house where no one knows how to cook it.
29 He says that he (not ride) that mare again, because she's dangerous.
30 Tom (not ride) in tomorrow's race, because he is too young. They don't allow riders under sixteen.
31 Whisky is absolutely necessary to me and I (not give) it up.
32 Jack (not drink) whisky this time next week, because he'll be in hospital and they won't give it to him there.
33 I (not open) the window. I dislike fresh air.

34 There is something on his mind, but he (not tell) me what it is.
35 The cat (not eat) fish so I have to buy meat for him.
36 He (not wear) uniform when you see him, because he'll be on leave then, and they don't wear uniform when they are on leave.

31 *will you?* and second person interrogative forms

A PEG 209 B

will you? often introduces a request or invitation, and sometimes a command. It is often used also to introduce questions about intentions when the situation requires an unpremeditated decision.

e.g. You can have either. Which will you have?
You've missed the last train. What will you do now?

For other types of intention, however, it is usually safer to use one of the other future forms: **be going to**, the present continuous or the future continuous (which is considered the most polite form).

Put the verbs in brackets into one of the four forms. When more than one answer is possible, this will be noted in the key.

1 Why are you taking all that bread with you? You (feed) the swans?
2 You (let) your flat again next summer?
3 You (light) the fire for me, please? Here are the matches.
4 You (wear) your new hat tomorrow?
5 I'd like to read that book. You (lend) it to me?
Yes, of course.
6 Shop assistant: You (come) this way, please?
7 You (have) something more to eat?
Yes, please, I'd like another sandwich.
8 You (have) anything more to eat?
No, because I haven't any more money.
9 You (study) computer programming at college?
10 You (speak) to Tom at the meeting tomorrow, do you think?
11 You (turn) off the TV, please? No one is watching it.
12 You (take) your exam now or in December?
13 You (listen) in to the concert this evening?
14 You (help) me with this, please? I can't open it.
15 I'm going to Brussels next week in my own plane. You (come) with me?
Thank you very much; I'd love to if you have room for me.

16 You (lend) me your typewriter for an hour? I want to type a letter.
17 You (meet) him at the station?
No, we never meet him. He doesn't like being met.
18 You (come) sailing with me this afternoon?
No, thank you, I don't like sailing.
19 You (have) some more wine? Yes, please.
20 I can't understand this letter. You (translate) it for me, Miss Pitt?
21 You (use) your camera this afternoon?
No, you can borrow it if you like.
22 You (go) to the tobacconist's?
Yes, I have to go to get some cigars for my father.
Then you (get) me twenty cigarettes?
23 You (come) to the Motor Show with me next Wednesday?
Thank you very much. I'd love to.
24 I'll be going abroad next week. Is there anything I can get you?
You (pass) through Paris?
Yes, I (spend) a few days there.
Then you (get) me some scent?
25 I see that you are putting your old henhouse in order. You (keep) hens?
26 I've just bought my tickets.
You (travel) by sea or air?
27 A lot of slates have just been left at your gate. You (repair) your roof?
28 You (hold) my parcels, please, while I put up my umbrella?
29 You (go) to Madeira as usual this summer?
30 You kindly (explain) why you didn't do what I told you?
31 You (recognize) him, do you think?
32 I've chosen a school for my son.
You (send) him to a public school or to a State school?
33 Passenger to bus conductor: You (tell) me where to get off, please?
34 You (go) by car? If so, would you give my brother a lift?
35 You (type) all night again? Because if so I think I'll go to a hotel.
36 Passenger to driver: You (look) where you are going? We nearly ran over that man.

32 *shall* and *will*

B PEG 202, 224–8, 233–4

shall is correct for the first person of the future tense (except when this tense is used to express intention), but in the affirmative and negative

will is very often used instead, i.e. we can say, 'I/we will' and 'I/we won't' instead of 'I/we shall' and 'I/we shan't.' In the interrogative **will** should not be used to replace **shall**.

There are some rather old-fashioned or formal constructions where **shall** is used with the 2nd or 3rd persons. Here **shall** cannot be replaced by **will**. Such constructions are usually avoided but a few examples have been given below.

Use **will** or **shall** to fill the spaces in the following sentences. Sometimes either could be used.

1 When you are in bed I . . . be at work.
2 Who'll help me? I . . .
3 We will unite to resist oppression, and tyrants . . . not triumph over us. (*We won't let them triumph.*)
4 What . . . we do now? Wait.
5 You've been a good child, and when we get home you . . . have a sweet.
6 Your father . . . hear of this. (*I'll certainly tell him.*)
7 . . . we go to the cinema? Yes, let's.
8 She . . . tell the same story over and over again. (*Obstinate insistence.*)
9 Club rule: Members . . . write the names of their guests in the book provided.
10 The world . . . know how unjustly we have been treated! (*We'll tell the world, etc.*)
11 Where . . . I be in six years' time, I wonder?
12 He . . . not come here again. (*He refuses.*)
13 He . . . not come here again. (*I won't let him come.*)
14 . . . you come to tea with me tomorrow?
Thank you very much, I'd love to.
15 This kind of snake . . . not bite unless it is startled.
16 . . . you have a cigarette? No, thanks, I don't smoke.
17 He . . . play his radio very loudly, which annoys me very much. (*Obstinate insistence.*)
18 By this time next year I . . . be earning my own living.
19 Who . . . take this letter to the post for me? I . . .
20 What . . . we do with all the food that's left over?
21 Do you know the way? No. Then I . . . show you.
22 Where . . . I put it? Put it behind the piano.
23 You . . . be astonished when you see this.
24 Yachts . . . go round the course, passing the marks in the correct order. (*Extract from Yacht Racing Rules.*)

25 When . . . you hear the result?
I . . . not hear for another week.
26 'I . . . not apologize', she said, stamping her foot.
27 Will you be good children while I'm out? We . . .
28 She . . . never do anything you tell her.
29 I . . . not be here next week.
30 I . . . not have to do any cooking for a month. I'm going to an hotel.
31 'You . . . have everything you want, my child', said the foolish woman. (*I'll give you everything you want.*)
32 . . . you really lend me your car? I . . . be very careful of it.
33 . . . you stand quite still for a moment, please?
34 . . . I put more salt in the stew?
35 A dog . . . obey his owner but a cat . . . not.
36 I . . . know whether you are telling the truth or not.

33 Time clauses

C PEG 203 C, 313

The future tense is not used in time clauses, the simple present tense being used instead.

Put the verbs in brackets into the correct tense (present or future).

1 When he (return) I'll give him the key.
2 He'll be ready as soon as you (be).
3 I'll stay in bed till the clock (strike) seven.
4 She will be delighted when she (hear) this.
5 When the laundry comes I (have) some clean handkerchiefs.
6 I shan't buy tomatoes till the price (come) down.
7 Stay here till the lights (turn) green.
8 When it (get) cold I'll light the fire.
9 The lift (not stop) until you press that button.
10 She'll have to behave better when she (go) to school.
11 When you look at yourself in the glass you (see) what I mean.
12 He (be) here before you go.
13 I (lend) you my cassette recorder whenever you want it.
14 He (wake) up when we turn the lights on.
15 He (ring) us up when he arrives in England?
16 He will wash up before he (go) to bed.
17 I won't come to London till the bus strike (be) over.
18 I (give) the children their dinner before he (come) home.

19 They will be astonished when they (see) how slowly he works.
20 I'll pay you when I (get) my cheque.
21 I (go) on doing it until he tells me to stop.
22 I'll buy that house when I (have) enough money.
23 You (fall) rapidly through the air till your parachute opens.
24 We'll have to stay here till the tide (go) out.
25 When the National Anthem (begin) the audience will stand up.
26 When the fog (lift) we'll be able to see where we are.
27 The refrigerator (continue) to make that noise till we have it repaired.
28 As soon as the holidays begin this beach (become) very crowded.
29 The car (not move) till you take the brake off.
30 The alarm bell (go on) ringing till you press this button.
31 As soon as she (learn) to type I'll get her a job.
32 Look before you (leap). (*proverb*)
33 We (have) to stay on this desert island till we can repair our boat.
34 Don't count on a salary increase before you actually (get) it.
35 When winter (begin) the swallows will fly away to a warmer country.
36 We can't make any decision till he (arrive) here.

34 The future perfect tense

C PEG 210

Put the verbs in brackets into the future perfect tense.

1 In a fortnight's time we (take) our exam.
2 I (finish) this book by tomorrow evening.
3 By this time tomorrow we (have) our injections.
4 By the end of next year I (be) here twenty-five years.
5 I'll still be here next summer but Tom (leave).
6 I (finish) this job in twenty minutes.
7 By next winter they (build) four houses in that field.
8 When we reach Valparaiso we (sail) all round the world.
9 At the rate he is going he (spend) all his money by the time he is twenty-one.
10 By this time next year I (save) £250.
11 By the time we get to the party everything (be) eaten.
12 The train (leave) before we reach the station.
13 If I continue with my diet I (lose) 10 kilos by the end of the month.
14 By the end of my university course I (attend) 1,200 lectures.

15 By the end of this week my illness (cost) me £100.
16 By the time that he leaves school his parents (spend) £6,000 on his education.
17 By the end of the term I (read) all twelve volumes.
18 When you come back I (finish) all the housework.
19 The police (hear) of the theft by this time.
20 We (drink) all that wine by the end of the year.
21 On the fourth of next month he (be) in prison for ten years.
22 When we reach Crewe we (do) half of the journey.
23 By the end of the month the new waitress (break) all the wine glasses.
24 If we don't hurry the sun (rise) before we reach the top.
25 I'm going to Hyde Park to hear the people making speeches.
You'll be too late. By the time you get there they (finish) their speeches and everybody (go) home.
26 By midnight he (be) unconscious for forty-eight hours.
27 By the end of the month 5,000 people (see) this exhibition.
28 By next April I (pay) £3,000 in income tax.
29 I suppose that when I come back in ten years' time all these old houses (be) pulled down.
30 On 21 October they (be) married for twenty-five years.
31 After this performance I (see) *Hamlet* twenty-two times.
32 The strike leader said, 'By midnight 500 men (come) out on strike.'
33 At your present rate you (burn) all that coal by the end of the month.
34 The treasurer said, 'By the end of the year all our debts (be paid) off.'
35 Tourist: We've only got five hours in Rome; we are leaving at six; but I'm sure that we (see) everything of importance by then.
36 Householder to Zoo: One of your elephants is in my garden eating my tomatoes.
Zoo official: The elephant keeper will be with you in half an hour.
Householder: Your elephant (eat) all my tomatoes by then.

35 Time clauses

B PEG 203 C, 313

The future perfect tense is not used in time clauses, the present perfect being used instead.

Put the verbs in brackets into the correct tense, using the future, present, or present perfect. Compare Nos. 1 to 5 with Nos. 1 to 5 in Exercise 34.

1 When we (take) our exam we'll have a holiday.
2 When I (finish) the book I'll lend it to you.
3 When we (have) our injections I expect we'll feel awful.
4 When I (be) here for a year I'll ask for a rise.
5 When Tom (go) I'll tell you a secret.
6 By the time he (get) back from his holiday the milkman will have left twenty-one bottles of milk outside his door.
7 Don't drive at more than 50 k.p.h. till your car (do) 4,000 kilometres.
8 When you (do) 4,000 kilometres you can drive it at 70 k.p.h.
9 When you open the safe you (see) a small black box.
10 When we (have) lunch we'll go for a walk.
11 When the bell rings I (take) the meat out of the oven.
12 I'll bolt all the doors before I (go) to bed.
13 When we (see) the cathedral we'll go to the museum.
14 We'll have to stay up this tree till the bull (go) away.
15 He (not let) you out till you have finished your homework.
16 As soon as I hear from him I (let) you know.
17 My father will be furious when he (see) what you have done.
18 You(not hear) the sound of the explosion till after you have seen the flash.
19 These gates will remain shut until the train (pass).
20 When he (sell) all his newspapers he'll go home.
21 We can't have a fire here until we (sweep) the chimney.
22 You (get) a shock when you open that box.
23 When you are twenty-five your father (give) you a latchkey.
24 Don't jump out of the aeroplane until the pilot (say) 'Go!'
25 I can't leave the country till the police (return) my passport.
26 When a bottle of champagne (be) opened for twenty-four hours the wine is not fit to drink.
27 Hotel receptionist: When you (sign) the hotel register the porter will show you your room.

28 You (not know) how good oysters are till you have tasted one.
29 That road will not be safe till the floods (subside).
30 When everybody (leave) the park the park-keeper will lock the gates.
31 When we have seen the Chamber of Horrors we (have) a cup of tea.
32 When you (have) something to eat you'll feel better.
33 I (stay) in court till the jury returns.
34 You cannot become a member of this club until you (make) a parachute descent.
35 When the boa constrictor (eat) his prey he will become very lethargic.
36 As soon as everybody has gone to bed the mice (come) out of their holes.

36 Conditional sentences: type 1

B PEG 215

Put the verbs in brackets into the correct tenses.

1 If I see him I (give) him a lift.
2 The table will collapse if you (stand) on it.
3 If you eat all that you (be) ill.
4 If I find your passport I (telephone) you at once.
5 The police (arrest) him if they catch him.
6 If you read in bad light you (ruin) your eyes.
7 Someone (steal) your car if you leave it unlocked.
8 What will happen if my parachute (not open)?
9 If you mow the grass I (give) you 50p.
10 I (lend) you my pearls if you promise to take care of them.
11 If you (not go) away I'll send for the police.
12 I (be) very angry if your dog bites me again.
13 If he (be) late we'll go without him.
14 She will be absolutely furious if she (hear) about this.
15 If you put on the kettle I (make) the tea.
16 If you give my dog a bone he (bury) it at once.
17 If we leave the car here it (not be) in anybody's way.
18 He'll be late for the train if he (not start) at once.
19 If you come late they (not let) you in.
20 If you tell any more lies I (be) very angry indeed.
21 Unless you work very hard you (not be) successful.

22 If I lend you £10 when you (repay) me?
23 We'll have to move upstairs if the river (rise) any higher.
24 If he (work) hard today can he have a holiday tomorrow?
25 Ice (turn) to water if you heat it.
26 If the house (catch) fire we can get out by the fire escape.
27 If you (not like) this one I'll bring you another.
28 Unless you are more careful you (have) an accident.
29 Tell him to ring me up if you (see) him.
30 If I tell you a secret, you (promise) not to tell it to anyone else?
31 If you (not believe) what I say, ask your mother.
32 You (buy) the house if you like it?
33 If you will kindly sit down I (make) enquiries for you.
34 Unless I have a quiet room I (not be able) to do any work.
35 Unless you pay him regularly he (not work) for you at all.
36 Should you require anything else please (ring) the bell for the attendant.

37 Conditional sentences: type 2

B PEG 216

Put the verbs in brackets into the correct tenses.

1 If I had a typewriter I (type) it myself.
2 If I knew his address I (give) it to you.
3 He (look) a lot better if he shaved more often.
4 If you played for lower stakes you (not lose) so much.
5 If he worked more slowly he (not make) so many mistakes.
6 More tourists (come) to this country if it had a better climate.
7 I shouldn't drink that wine if I (be) you.
8 If I were sent to prison, you (visit) me?
9 If someone gave you a helicopter, what you (do) with it?
10 I (buy) shares in that company if I had some money.
11 If he (clean) his windscreen he'd be able to see where he was going.
12 If you drove your car into the river, you (be able) to get out?
13 Conversation would become impossible if everyone (say) exactly what he thought.
14 If I (win) a big prize in a lottery I'd give up my job.
15 What you (do) if a burglar came into your room at night?
16 I could tell you what this means if I (know) Greek.
17 If everyone gave £1 we (have) enough.

18 He might get fat if he (stop) smoking.
19 If he knew that it was dangerous he (not come).
20 If you saw somebody drowning, what you (do)?
21 I (be) ruined if I bought her everything she asked for.
22 If you slept under a mosquito net you (not be) stung so often.
23 I could get a job easily if I (have) a degree.
24 If she (do) her hair differently she might look quite nice.
25 If we had more rain our crops (grow) better.
26 The whole machine (fall) to pieces if you removed that screw.
27 I (keep) a horse if I could afford it.
28 I'd ask him to dinner more often if he (be) more amusing.
29 If you moved the bed out of your hall it (be) easier to get into the house.
30 I (offer) to help if I thought that I'd be any use.
31 What would you do if the lift (get) stuck between two floors?
32 It (make) a great difference to the room if you painted each wall a different colour.
33 I (not go) there if I were you.
34 If you knew that you had only six weeks more to live, how you (spend) those six weeks?
35 You wouldn't have so much trouble with your car if you (have) it serviced regularly.
36 I'd climb over the wall if there (not be) so much broken glass on top of it.

38 Conditional sentences: type 3

B PEG 217

Put the verbs in brackets into the correct tenses.

1 If I had known that you were in hospital I (visit) you.
2 If the captain had been more careful his ship (not be) sunk.
3 If you (arrive) ten minutes earlier you would have got a seat.
4 You would have seen my garden at its best if you (be) here last week.
5 But for his quickness I (be) killed.
6 I shouldn't have believed it if I (not see) it with my own eyes.
7 If he had slipped he (fall) 500 metres.
8 If he had asked you, you (accept)?
9 The burglars (not do) so much damage if you hadn't locked all the drawers.

10 If I (know) that you were coming I'd have baked a cake.
11 I (offer) to help him if I had realized that he was ill.
12 If you had left that wasp alone it (not sting) you.
13 If I (realize) what a bad driver you were I wouldn't have come with you.
14 If I had realized that the traffic lights were red I (stop).
15 But for the fog we (reach) our destination ages ago.
16 If you had told me that he never paid his debts I (not lend) him the money.
17 If you (not sneeze) he wouldn't have known that we were there.
18 If you (put) some mustard in the sandwiches they would have tasted better.
19 The hens (not get) into the house if you had shut the door.
20 If he had known that the river was dangerous he (not try) to swim across it.
21 If you (speak) more slowly he might have understood you.
22 If he had known the whole story he (not be) so angry.
23 I shouldn't have eaten it if I (know) that there was ginger in it.
24 If I (try) again I think that I would have succeeded.
25 You (not get) into trouble if you had obeyed my instructions.
26 If you hadn't been in such a hurry you (not put) sugar into the sauce instead of salt.
27 If I (be) ready when he called he would have taken me with him.
28 I (catch) the train quite easily if I hadn't been wearing tight new shoes.
29 If she had listened to my directions she (not turn) down the wrong street.
30 If you (look) at the engine for a moment you would have seen what was missing.
31 Rome (be captured) by her enemies if the geese hadn't cackled.
32 He would have been arrested if he (try) to leave the country.
33 I (take) a taxi if I had realized that it was such a long way.
34 You (save) me a lot of trouble if you had told me where you were going.
35 They would have forced their way into the house if I (not call) for help.
36 If he had put out his pipe before putting it in his pocket he (not burn) a hole in his coat.

39 Conditional sentences: mixed types

A PEG 215–17

Put the verbs in brackets into the correct tenses.

1 If you (find) a skeleton in the cellar don't mention it to anyone.
2 If you pass your examination we (have) a celebration.
3 What (happen) if I press this button?
4 I should have voted for her if I (have) a vote then.
5 If you go to Paris where you (stay)?
6 If someone offered to buy you one of those rings, which you (choose)?
7 The flight may be cancelled if the fog (get) thick.
8 If the milkman (come) tell him to leave two pints.
9 Someone (sit) on your glasses if you leave them there.
10 You would play better bridge if you (not talk) so much.
11 What I (do) if I hear the burglar alarm?
12 If you (read) the instructions carefully you wouldn't have answered the wrong question.
13 I could repair the roof myself if I (have) a long ladder.
14 Unless they turn that radio off I (go) mad.
15 If you saw a Brontosaurus walking down Oxford Street what you (do)?
16 We'll have a long way to walk if we (run) out of petrol here.
17 If you shake that bottle of port it (not be) fit to drink.
18 I'll probably get lost unless he (come) with me.
19 You (not have) so many accidents if you drove more slowly.
20 If you (wear) a false beard nobody would have recognized you.
21 If she (leave) the fish there the cat will get it.
22 Unless they leave a lamp beside that hole in the road somebody (fall) into it.
23 You'll get pneumonia if you (not change) your wet clothes.
24 If I had known that you couldn't eat octopus I (not buy) it.
25 If they (hang) that picture lower people would be able to see it.
26 She (be able) to walk faster if her shoes hadn't such high heels.
27 I (bring) you some beer if I had known that you were thirsty.
28 If you had touched that electric cable you (be) electrocuted.
29 If the story hadn't been true the newspaper (not print) it.
30 I (not buy) things on the instalment system if I were you.
31 Dial 999 if you (want) Police, Ambulance, or Fire Brigade.
32 You (not be) any use to me unless you learn to type.

33 If anyone attacked me, my dog (jump) at his throat.
34 If he were in he (answer) the phone.
35 The ship would have run aground if the pilot (make) one mistake.
36 I shouldn't have taken your umbrella if I (know) that it was the only one you had.

40 Conditional sentences: mixed types

A PEG 215–17

Finish these sentences, taking care to use the correct tenses.

1 If he had taken my advice . . .
2 If you ate less . . .
3 We'll send for the doctor if . . .
4 If she practised more . . .
5 If there isn't enough wine in that bottle . . .
6 If you had checked the petrol before we started . . .
7 This clock wouldn't have run down if . . .
8 Try on the blue one if . . .
9 If these gates are locked . . .
10 If we leave before breakfast . . .
11 If the river rises any higher . . .
12 Her life might have been saved if . . .
13 If the volcano starts erupting . . .
14 The grass would look better if . . .
15 Unless it is a nice day . . .
16 If you don't put enough stamps on a letter, the person who gets it . . .
17 He would lend it to you if . . .
18 Unless this hotel gets another cook . . .
19 If the storm becomes worse . . .
20 If your uncle sees you . . .
21 If you tried to climb it without a guide . . .
22 If you didn't shake the camera so much, your photographs . . .
23 I'd have brought my coat . . .
24 If he cut his hair more often . . .
25 He would have given her diamonds if . . .
26 If you had asked his permission . . .
27 If the fire had been noticed earlier . . .
28 If you had any sense . . .
29 You would have been angry if . . .

30 If he had put the flowers into water at once . . .
31 I should have ordered more coal if . . .
32 If you leave the gate open . . .
33 You will have to go to the dentist if . . .
34 He would have been drowned if . . .
35 If I'd had a car . . .
36 If the telephone rings while I'm in my bath . . .

3 Gerund, infinitive and participles

41 Infinitive with or without *to*

C PEG 243

Insert **to** where necessary before the infinitives in brackets.

1 He made me (do) it all over again.
2 She can (sing) quite well.
3 He will be able (swim) very soon.
4 I used (live) in a caravan.
5 You ought (go) today. It may (rain) tomorrow.
6 You needn't (say) anything. Just nod your head and he will (understand).
7 I want (see) the house where our president was born.
8 He made her (repeat) the message.
9 May I (use) your phone?
10 You needn't (ask) for permission; you can (use) it whenever you like.
11 If you want (get) there before dark you should (start) at once.
12 I couldn't (remember) his address.
13 You'll be able (do) it yourself when you are older.
14 Would you like (go) now or shall we (wait) till the end?
15 They won't let us (leave) the Customs shed till our luggage has been examined.
16 How dare you (open) my letters!
17 She persuaded him (wait) a little longer.
18 I used (smoke) forty cigarettes a day.
19 Will you help me (move) the bookcase?
20 He wouldn't let my baby (play) with his gold watch.
21 They refused (accept) the bribe.
22 He is expected (arrive) in a few days.
23 Please let me (know) your decision as soon as possible.
24 He made us (wait) for hours.
25 Could you (tell) me the time, please?
26 We must (send) him a telegram.
27 I let him (go) early as he wanted (meet) his wife.

28 Where would you like (have) lunch?
29 You can (leave) your dog with us if you don't (want) (take) him with you.
30 I'd like him (go) to a university but I can't (make) him (go).
31 We could (go) to a concert, unless you'd prefer (visit) a museum.
32 You seem (know) this area very well.
Yes, I used (live) here.
33 The kidnappers told the parents (not inform) the police, and the parents didn't dare (disobey).
34 Need I (come)? I'd much rather (stay) at home.
35 You can (take) a horse to water but you can't (make) him (drink). (*proverb*)
36 I'm sorry (disappoint) you but I can't (let) you (have) any more money till the end of the month.

42 Infinitive with or without *to*

B PEG 243

Insert **to** where necessary before the infinitives in brackets. (In some of the sentences a present participle could be used instead of an infinitive. These alternatives will be noted in the key.)

1 It is easy (be) wise after the event.
2 Do you (wish) (make) a complaint?
3 We don't (want) anybody (know) that we are here.
4 If you can't (remember) his number you'd better (look) it up.
5 I want her (learn) Esperanto; I think everybody ought (know) it.
6 He is said (be) the best surgeon in the country.
7 Visitors are asked (not feed) the animals.
8 Could I (see) Mr Pitt, please?
I'm afraid Mr Pitt isn't in. Would you like (speak) to his secretary?
9 It's better (travel) hopefully than (arrive). (*proverb*)
10 He should (know) how (use) the film projector, but if he doesn't you had better (show) him.
11 If the baby is a boy there is (be) a salute of 21 guns.
12 I heard the door (open) and saw a shadow (move) across the floor.
13 He tried (make) me (believe) that he was my stepbrother.
14 As we seem (have missed) the train we may as well (go) back to the house.
15 I felt the house (shake) with the explosion.
16 He told me (try) (come) early.

17 Before he let us (go) he made us (promise) (not tell) anyone what we had seen.
18 Would you (like) (come) in my car?
No, thanks, I'd rather (walk).
19 I advised him (ask) the bus conductor (tell) him where (get) off.
20 It is better (put) your money in a bank than (keep) it under your bed in an old stocking.
21 She expects her husband (pay) all the household expenses although she has a good job, too.
22 The bank robbers made the cashier (show) them how (open) the safe.
23 If you knew he was wrong, why didn't you (say) something?
I didn't like (say) anything because he always gets angry if you contradict him.
24 It's better (be) sure than sorry.
25 What do you (want) me (tell) him?
Tell him that any time he cares (call) I shall be delighted (discuss) the matter with him.
26 Did you remember (give) him the money?
No, I didn't, I still have it in my pocket; but I'll (see) him tonight and I promise (not forget) this time.
27 I saw the driver (open) his window and (throw) a box into the bushes.
28 That is far too heavy for one person (carry); let me (help) you.
29 I was afraid (pick) up the revolver as I don't know how (handle) firearms.
30 I saw the plane (crash) into the hill and (burst) into flames.
31 There is nothing (do) but (wait) till somebody comes (let) us out.
32 He heard a cock (crow) in a neighbouring village.
33 You may as well (tell) us the truth. It will (be) easy (check) your story.
34 The American said he had seen nine presidents (come) and (go).
He must (be) a very old man.
35 It is up to you (learn) the laws of your own country.
36 Would you rather (be) more stupid than you look or (look) more stupid than you are?

43 Infinitive represented by *to*

C PEG 253

In each of the following pairs of sentences an infinitive used in the first sentence is repeated in the second. Read the sentences, expressing this second infinitive by **to** only. Note that where the second infinitive has an object, this word/phrase must be omitted.

e.g. Why didn't you tell me the truth the first time?
I meant to tell you the truth but I was too frightened.
I meant to but I was too frightened.

1 Did you visit the Pyramids?
No, I wanted to visit them but there wasn't time.
2 Why do you wear dark glasses?
I have to wear them; I have weak eyes.
3 Do you smoke?
No, I used to smoke but I don't now.
4 Would you like to go to the theatre tonight?
Yes, I'd love to go to the theatre.
5 Why didn't you pay the bill for him?
I offered to pay it but he refused.
6 Have you put the car in the garage?
No, but I'm just going to put it there.
7 I want you two to apologize to each other.
Well, I am willing to apologize if he apologizes first.
8 Did you reserve seats on the train?
No, I tried to reserve them but they had all been booked already.
9 Did you answer the letter?
No, I intended to answer it but I'm afraid I forgot.
10 Why didn't you hit him?
I was afraid to hit him.
11 I'd love to spend a night in a haunted room.
I'd hate to spend a night in a haunted room.
12 Why didn't you ask your father for the money?
I didn't like to ask him.
13 Did you get a chance to fly the aeroplane yourself?
No, I wanted to fly it but the pilot wouldn't let me.
14 Why doesn't he punish his boys when they disobey him?
He often threatens to punish them but he never actually does so.
15 Why didn't he repair the car himself?
He wasn't able to repair it.

16 I used to drink whisky with my meals.
I used to drink whisky with my meals also but I don't now.

17 Did you buy sausages?
No, I meant to buy them but I forgot.

18 Why doesn't he try again?
He doesn't want to try again.

19 You should visit the Prado when you are in Madrid.
Yes, I intend to visit it.

20 Why doesn't he play games?
His mother doesn't want him to play games.

21 You ought to stop work now.
Yes, I am just going to stop.

22 Why do some jockeys carry extra weights?
They are obliged to carry them by the regulations.

23 Did he help you?
No, I asked him to help me but he said he hadn't time.

24 You should have thanked her before you left.
I meant to thank her but when I was going I couldn't find her anywhere.

25 Why did she put parsley in the soup?
I told her to put it in.

26 Why didn't he report it to the police?
He was afraid to report it. He didn't think they'd believe him.

27 Why did he drive so fast?
He had to drive fast; otherwise he'd have missed his train.

28 You used to like rice pudding.
Yes, I know I used to like it but I don't now.

29 Why didn't you buy the car?
I was advised not to buy it.

30 I hope the children won't go near the water.
I warned them not to go near it.

31 Why are we trying to get planning permission?
We have to get planning permission. It is the law.

32 I meant to work hard.
I know you meant to work hard but you didn't.

33 Do the boys tidy their own rooms?
They are supposed to tidy them but they don't always.

34 Why didn't he call the police?
He wasn't able to call them. His telephone line had been cut.

35 Why did you move your car?
The policeman told me to move it.

36 Why did you bring your mother-in-law? I particularly asked you not to bring her.

44 Indirect commands expressed by object + infinitive

C PEG 301

Indirect commands are normally expressed by **tell**, **order**, **ask**, **beg**, **warn**, **advise** etc., with the person addressed and the infinitive. Change the following direct commands into indirect commands using this construction. Remember that the person addressed is often not mentioned in a direct command,

e.g. He said, 'Go away',

but must be mentioned in an indirect command,

e.g. He told me (Tom/us/them, etc) to go away.

1 'Put some coal on the fire,' he said to her.
2 'Shut the door, Tom,' she said.
3 'Lend me your pen for a moment,' I said to Mary.
4 'Don't read in bad light, boys,' I said.
5 'Don't believe everything you hear,' he advised me.
6 'Please fill up this form,' the secretary said.
7 'Don't hurry,' I called to them.
8 'Don't touch that switch, Mary,' I said.
9 'Put your hands up,' the raiders told the bank clerk.
10 'Please do as I say,' he begged me.
11 'Help your mother, Peter,' Mr Pitt said.
12 'Don't make too much noise, children,' he said.
13 'Do whatever you like,' she said to us.
14 'Don't miss your train,' she warned them.
15 'Read it before you sign it,' he said to his client.
16 'Sing it again,' he asked her.
17 'Brush your hair, Robert,' his mother said.
18 'Buy a new car,' I advised him.
19 'Don't drive too fast,' she begged him.
20 'Don't forget to listen to the first programme in the new series at eight o'clock,' the announcer said to his listeners.
21 'Come to the cinema with me,' he asked her.
22 'Cook it in butter,' I advised her.

23 'Don't touch the gates, madam,' said the lift operator.
24 'Don't argue with me,' the teacher said to the boy.
25 'Pull as hard as you can,' he said to him.
26 'Send for the Fire Brigade,' the manager said to the porter.
27 'Don't lend her anything,' he advised us.
28 'Make a list of what you want,' she told us.
29 'Look at the paper,' he said to her.
30 'Stand clear of the doors,' a voice warned the people on the platform.
31 'See if you can find any eggs,' my aunt said to me.
32 'Don't go alone,' I warned her.
33 'Pay at the cash desk,' the shop assistant said to the customer.
34 'Don't point, children,' she said.
35 'Put the ladder against the wall,' I said to the man.
36 'Think well before you answer,' the detective warned her.

45 Indirect commands expressed by object + infinitive

C PEG 301

In the following exercise, the verb **said** has been used throughout, but the student should use the verbs mentioned in the note to the previous exercise and should also supply a suitable indirect object.

1 'Come down at once,' my father said.
2 'Be patient,' the Prime Minister said.
3 'Buy the large tin,' the shopkeeper said.
4 'Don't bathe here,' I said.
5 'Turn right at the next cross-roads,' the policeman said.
6 'Go to the other counter,' the clerk said.
7 'Have your passports ready,' a voice said.
8 'Stand at ease,' the sergeant said.
9 'Translate the first twenty lines,' the teacher said.
10 'Listen to the birds,' I said.
11 'Don't believe everything she tells you,' he said.
12 'Keep moving,' the policeman said.
13 'Look everywhere,' he said.
14 'Never lend money to people you don't know,' he said to his son.
15 'Put your luggage on the scales, please,' the clerk said.
16 'Take a deep breath,' the doctor said.

17 'Don't spend it all at once,' his employer said.
18 'Tell me all about it,' she said.
19 'Look around you,' I said.
20 'Give me ten pence,' the child said.
21 'Open your suitcases,' the Customs officer said.
22 'Don't waste time,' my mother always said.
23 'Please pass the salt,' he said.
24 'Dismount,' the riding instructor said.
25 'Put some crumbs on the window-sill for the birds,' she said.
26 'Come in out of the rain,' I said.
27 'Don't put your hands near the bars,' the zoo keeper said.
28 'Don't lean your bicycle against my window,' the grocer said.
29 'Cross the line by the footbridge,' the porter said.
30 'Don't shout into the telephone,' my mother said.
31 'Meet me here at the same time tomorrow,' he said.
32 'Don't decide in a hurry. Think it over,' I said.
33 'Please help me to mend it,' she said.
34 'Open a tin of soup,' I said.
35 'Please mend the puncture,' the driver said.
36 'Don't put the wine near the fire,' I said.

46 *too/enough/so . . . as* with infinitive

C PEG 251

Combine each of the following pairs of sentences into one sentence using **too/enough** with infinitive.

e.g. It is very cold. We can't go out.
It is too cold for us to go out.
He is strong. He can carry it.
He is strong enough to carry it.

Rewrite numbers 3, 20, and 35 using **so . . . as** with infinitive. (**enough** with infinitive could also be used here, while **so . . . as** could replace **enough** in numbers 9, 24, and 29. These alternatives are given in the key.)

1 You are very young. You can't have a front-door key.
2 It is very cold. We can't bathe.
3 Would you be very kind and answer this letter by return?
4 I am rather old. I can't wear that kind of hat.
5 The rope wasn't strong. It couldn't support the two men.

6 He hadn't much money. He couldn't live on it. (*Omit* it)
7 He was furious. He couldn't speak.
8 The fire isn't very hot. It won't boil a kettle.
9 Tom was very foolish. He told lies to the police.
10 You are quite thin. You could slip between the bars.
11 He is very ill. He can't eat anything.
12 Our new car is very wide. It won't get through those gates.
13 The floor wasn't strong. We couldn't dance on it. (*Omit* it)
14 I was terrified. I couldn't move.
15 The bull isn't big. He couldn't harm you.
16 The coffee isn't strong. It won't keep us awake.
17 The river is deep. We can't wade it. (*Omit* it)
18 I am quite old. I could be your father.
19 I am very rich. I could buy your whole hotel.
20 Would you be very good and forward my letters while I am away?
21 The ice is quite thick. We can walk on it. (*Omit* it)
22 He was very drunk. He couldn't answer my question.
23 It is very cold. We can't have breakfast in the garden.
24 He was extremely rash. He set off up the mountain in a thick fog.
25 We aren't very high. We can't see the summit.
26 You aren't very old. You can't understand these things.
27 He was very snobbish. He wouldn't talk to any of us.
28 The package is very thick. I can't push it through the letterbox. (*Omit* it)
29 He was very curious. He opened the letter.
30 The dog was impatient. He wouldn't remain at the rathole.
31 My rats are very clever. They can't be caught in traps.
32 It was very dark. We couldn't see the signpost.
33 It was very hot. You could fry an egg on the pavement.
34 The oranges were very bitter. We couldn't eat them. (*Omit* them)
35 Would you be very kind and turn down the gas fire a little?
36 It was rather cloudy. We couldn't see the eclipse properly.

47 Various infinitive constructions

A PEG 245–51

Replace the group of words in italics by an infinitive or an infinitive construction.

e.g. It is important *that he should understand* this.
It is important for him to understand this.

He was the first man *who arrived.*
He was the first man to arrive.

1 The captain was the last man *who left* the ship.
2 He got to the top *and was very disappointed when he found* that someone else had reached it first.
3 *The committee have decided to send you* to Paris. (You (go) to Paris, *omit* the committee have decided to send)
4 Would you be *very* kind *and* lend me your umbrella?
5 There are a lot of sheets *that need mending.*
6 I was astonished *when I heard* that he had left the country.
7 It is better *that he should hear* it from you.
8 *I was rude* to him, *which was stupid.* (It was stupid . . .)
9 If he had another child *with whom he could play* he would be happier.
10 It is necessary *that everyone should know* the truth.
11 There was no place *where we could sit.*
12 He put his hand into his pocket *and was astonished when he found* that his wallet wasn't there.
13 *He rushed* into the burning house, *which* was very brave of him. (It was very brave . . .)
14 I can't go to the party; I have nothing *that I can wear.*
15 *It is expected that he will broadcast* a statement tonight. (He is expected . . .)
16 I want a kitchen *where (= in which) I can cook.*
17 He reached the station exhausted *and was very disappointed when he learnt* that the train had just left.
18 Haven't you anything *with which you could open it*?
19 *It seems that the crime was committed* by a left-handed man. (The crime seems . . . *Use perfect infinitive passive*)
20 Is *it* likely *that he will arrive* before six? (Is he . . .)
21 I was *on the point of leaving* the house when the phone rang.
22 *This is the plan: someone will meet you* at the station . . . (You . . . (be met) at the station)
23 She is anxious *that they should have* every possible advantage.
24 *It is said that* he was a brilliant scientist. (He is said . . .)
25 The strikers decided *that the strike should continue.*
26 Would you be *very kind and translate* this for me?
27 It is advisable *that we should leave* the house separately.
28 *You signed* the document without reading it, *which was very stupid.* (It was stupid . . .)
29 *It is said that she has* a frightful temper. (She . . .)

30 He was the first man *who swam* the Channel.
31 *They believe that he is* honest. (He . . .)
32 *It appears that he was killed* with a blunt instrument. (He appears . . . *Use passive infinitive*)
33 He was the only one *who realized* the danger.
34 *It is said that the earth was* originally part of the sun. (The earth . . .)
35 He took out his spare wheel and *was very disappointed when he discovered* that that tyre was also punctured.
36 *It is said that the murderer is hiding* in the woods near your house.

48 Infinitive used to express purpose

B PEG 308

Combine each of the following pairs of sentences into one sentence using **so as/in order** where necessary.

e.g. He sent me to Spain. He wanted me to learn Spanish.
He sent me to Spain to learn Spanish.
He turned out the light. He didn't want to waste electricity.
He turned out the light so as not to waste electricity.

1 I am buying paint. I want to paint my hall door.
2 He tied a knot in his handkerchief. He hoped that this would remind him to meet the train.
3 He opened the lions' cage. He intended to feed the lions.
4 He left his rifle outside. He didn't want to frighten his wife.
5 He has a box. He plans to put his savings in it. (*Omit* it)
6 We had no cups but he gave us coconut shells. He said we could drink out of them. (*Omit* them)
7 He rushed into the burning house. He wanted to save the child.
8 He read only for short periods each day. He didn't want to strain his eyes.
9 They got up very early. They wanted to get to the top of the hill before sunrise.
10 He rang the bell. He wanted to tell us that dinner was ready.
11 We must keep our gloves on. We don't want to get frost-bitten.
12 The farmer put a scarecrow up in the field. He wanted to frighten the birds.
13 I took off my shoes. I didn't want to make any noise.
14 Before the carpenter came she covered the floor with polythene sheeting. She wanted to protect the carpet.

15 The boys are collecting sticks. They intend to put them on the fire. (*Omit* them)
16 He was playing very softly. He didn't want to disturb anyone.
17 I am sending him to the U.S.A. I want him to study electronics there.
18 I sent him out of the room. I wanted to discuss his progress with his headmaster.
19 He fixed a metal ladder to the wall below his window. He wanted to be able to escape if there was a fire.
20 He changed his address constantly. He wanted to elude the police.
21 The police have barricaded the main streets. They want to prevent the demonstrators from marching through the town.
22 They evacuated everybody from the danger zone. They wanted to reduce the risk.
23 I am learning Greek. I wish to read Homer.
24 He sent his children to his sister's house. He wanted them to watch the television programme.
25 He sent his children to their aunt's house. He wanted some peace.
26 The town council has forbidden coal fires. They are trying to keep the air clean.
27 They employed a detective. They wanted to learn what I did in the evenings.
28 I am saving up. I want to buy a helicopter.
29 He coughed. He wanted to warn them that he was coming.
30 You should take your holidays in June. In this way you would avoid the rush.
31 I keep my hens in a field surrounded by wire netting. I want to protect them against the foxes.
32 I am learning skiing at an indoor school. I want to be able to ski when I get to Switzerland.
33 The workmen left red lights near the hole. They wanted to warn motorists.
34 He invented a wife and six children. By this trick he hoped to avoid paying income tax.
35 Some women tint their hair when it goes grey. They want to look younger.
36 He didn't tell her he was going in the rocket. He didn't want to alarm her.

49 Clauses and phrases of purpose

A PEG 309

The most useful construction here is (i) a purpose clause introduced by **so that**. But (ii) this can sometimes be replaced by an infinitive phrase consisting of **prevent/avoid** + gerund or **allow/enable/let/make** etc. + infinitive.

e.g. The two sentences: *He rumpled the bedclothes; he wanted to make me think he had slept in the bed* could be combined: *He rumpled the bedclothes so that I would/should think he had slept* etc. or: . . . *to make me think he had slept* etc.

(iii) An **in case** clause is useful when we mention the possible future action we are taking precautions against:

e.g. *Don't let him play with scissors; he may cut himself* could be expressed *Don't let him play with scissors in case he cuts himself.*

Sometimes an **in case** clause can be replaced by a negative purpose clause.

1 He killed the men who helped him to bury the treasure. He wanted nobody but himself to know where it was.
2 Put the cork back. Someone may knock the bottle over.
3 The airfield authorities have put arc lights over the damaged runway. They want repair work to continue day and night.
4 The girl packed the vase in polyester foam. She didn't want it to get broken in the post.
5 He wore a false beard. He didn't want anyone to recognize him.
6 She built a high wall round her garden. She didn't want her fruit to be stolen.
7 They talked in whispers. They didn't want me to overhear them.
8 You ought to take some serum with you. You may get bitten by a snake.
9 Aeroplanes carry parachutes. The crew can escape in case of fire.
10 I am insuring my life. I want my children to have something to live on if I am killed.
11 Please shut the gate. I don't want the cows to get out of the field.
12 He telephoned from a public call-box. He didn't want the call to be traced to his own address.
13 I am putting nets over my strawberry plants. I don't want the birds to eat all the strawberries.

14 We keep a spade in the house. There may be a heavy fall of snow in the night.
15 We put bars on the lower windows. We didn't want anyone to climb in.
16 You should carry a jack in your car. You may have a puncture.
17 We built the roof with a steep slope. We wanted the snow to slide off easily.
18 The notices are written in several languages. The government wants everyone to understand them.
19 I put my address on my dog's collar. I want anyone who finds him to know where he comes from.
20 She tied a bell round her cat's neck. She wanted the birds to know when he was approaching.
21 Bring your gun with you. We may be attacked.
22 I have put wire over my chimney-pots. I don't want birds to build nests in them.
23 Write your name in the book. He may forget who lent it to him.
24 He chained up the lioness at night. He didn't want her to frighten anyone.
25 Don't put on any more coal. The chimney may catch fire.
26 The burglar cut the telephone wires. He didn't want me to call the police.
27 Take a torch with you. It may be dark before you get back.
28 The manufacturers have made the taps of their new gas cooker very stiff. They don't want young children to be able to turn them on.
29 Don't let the baby play with my glasses. He may break them.
30 The debate on education has been postponed. The government want to discuss the latest crisis.
31 If someone knocks at the door at night don't open it. It may be the escaped convict.
32 The policeman stopped the traffic every few minutes. He wanted the pedestrians to be able to cross the road.
33 He had a telephone installed in his car. He wanted his secretary to be able to contact him whenever necessary.
34 Never let children play with matches. They may set themselves on fire.
35 As he went through the forest Bill marked the trees. He wanted the rest of the party to know which way he had gone.
36 Turn down the oven. We don't want the meat to burn while we are out.

50 Perfect infinitive used with auxiliary verbs

A PEG 255

Use the perfect infinitive of the verb in italics with the appropriate auxiliary verb. Phrases underlined should not be repeated, but their meaning should be expressed by the auxiliary + perfect infinitive.

e.g. It is possible that he *telephoned* while we were out.
He may have telephoned while we were out.
You (*thank*) him for his present but you didn't.
You should have thanked him for his present.

1 I realized that my house was on fire.
That (*be*) a terrible moment.
2 I saw a ghost last night.
You (*not see*) a ghost; there aren't any ghosts. You (*dream*) it.
3 It is possible that a child *broke* the window.
4 You *carried* it yourself, which was not necessary.
5 I've had a toothache for two days.
You (*go*) to the dentist when it started.
6 There (*be*) motor-cycle races on the sands but as it is so wet they have been cancelled.
7 As I was standing in the hall your dog bit me.
It (*not be*) my dog; he was with me all day. It (*be*) my brother's dog.
8 I feel terribly ill today.
You (*not eat*) those mushrooms yesterday. Mushrooms don't agree with you.
9 I wonder why he didn't answer?
Possibly he *didn't understand* the question.
10 I *gave* him a tip, which was not necessary.
11 The prisoner (*escape*) this way, for here are his footprints.
12 You *lied* to him, which was wrong.
13 I didn't recognize the voice at the other end of the line.
It (*be*) my elder sister; she is often at home at that time. It (*not be*) my youngest sister as she is abroad.
14 Someone (*cook*) a meal here lately; the stove is still hot.
15 I've brought my own sandwiches.
You (*not bring*) them. I have enough for two.
16 The burglar went straight to the safe although it was hidden behind a picture.
Someone (*tell*) him where it was.

17 The president (*unveil*) the statue, but he is ill so his wife is doing it instead.
18 The plane is late; I wonder what has happened?
Possibly it *was* delayed by fog.
19 I have never met him.
You (*meet*) him; he lives next door to you.
20 I (*do*) it. (It was my duty to do it, but I didn't.)
21 He (*not catch*) the 9.20 train because he didn't leave home till 9.25.
22 I *opened* it, which was unnecessary.
23 The police were here while we were out.
Someone (*betray*) us.
24 I *drove* at 80 miles an hour, which was wrong.
25 When I was your age I (*climb*) that mountain, (but I didn't).
26 If a policeman had seen me climbing through your window he (*ask*) me what I was doing.
27 He said that censorship of news was ridiculous and it (*abolish*) years ago. (passive verb)
28 You *boiled* so many eggs; but there are only four of us.
29 She (*play*) the chief part in the film, but she quarrelled with the director, so he engaged someone else.
30 This poem (*be*) written by Keats, but I am not certain.
31 He (*take*) off his hat in the theatre, (but he didn't).
32 People used to walk twenty miles to do their shopping.
They (*have*) a lot of energy in those days.
33 One day he went for a walk up a mountain and never came back.
He (*fall*) over a precipice.
34 I just pressed lightly on the pane and my hand went through.
The glass (*be*) very thin.
35 You *translated* it into French, which wasn't necessary.
36 You *looked* at the new moon through glass. It is most unlucky.

51 Perfect infinitive used with auxiliaries and some other verbs

A PEG 255

Instructions: as for Exercise 50, but where two verbs in italics are placed side by side, put the second verb into the perfect infinitive and the first into an appropriate tense.

e.g. This palace (*say*) (*build*) in three years.
This palace is said to have been built in three years.

1 She (*marry*) my brother but she was killed in a plane crash a month before the wedding date.
2 You *repeated* it, which was unnecessary.
3 There (*seem*) (*be*) a fight here. Everything is smashed to bits.
4 We (*set*) out today, but the weather is so bad that we decided to postpone our start till tomorrow.
5 I thought they were mushrooms.
You (*not eat*) them unless you were sure. They (*be*) poisonous.
6 He learnt the language in six months.
He (*work*) very hard.
7 I *brought* my umbrella, which was unnecessary.
8 I (*like*) (*bathe*) but there wasn't time.
9 I've forgotten the address. I (*write*) it down (but I didn't).
10 If I'd known your house was so cold I (*not come*).
11 Why did you put pepper in it?
But I didn't.
Then it (*be*) Mary. She puts pepper in everything.
12 Who gave you my address?
I don't remember. It (*be*) Tom.
It (*not be*) Tom; he doesn't know it.
13 You *bought* flowers but we have plenty in the garden.
14 After two years of his teaching she knew absolutely nothing.
He (*not be*) a good teacher.
15 My sister has just come back from abroad. She (*seem*) (*enjoy*) her trip very much.
16 Life (*be*) very uncomfortable in the Stone Age.
17 You (*stand*) still when you were being photographed, (but you didn't).
18 I (*go*) to a foreign university but the war prevented it.
19 I (*like*) (*photograph*) it but I had no more film.
20 There (*be*) a bad accident here. Look at all the broken glass.
21 It is possible that prehistoric cave drawings *were* connected with religion.
22 I have been driving for 20 years.
You (*not drive*) for 20 years. You are only 30 now.
23 It (*take*) years to dig the Suez Canal.
24 He walked past me without speaking.
He (*not recognize*) you. He is very short-sighted.
25 I (*like*) (*go*) to the match but the tickets were all sold.
26 He says he saw you at the theatre yesterday.
He (*not see*) me. I wasn't there.
27 This picture may be a fake; on the other hand it (*be*) painted by one

of the Dutch masters.

28 It is possible that the fire in the ship *was started* by a bomb.

29 She walked 300 miles, carrying her child.
She (*have*) great courage.

30 It is possible that he (*read*) it in the papers.
He (*not read*) it. He can't read. Someone (*tell*) him.

31 I told them to meet me under the clock but they didn't turn up. Perhaps they *were waiting* under the wrong clock. There are two in the station.

32 He told me his name was Johnson.
You (*mishear*) him. His name is Jones.

33 I said that I couldn't find my pen and he said that perhaps somebody *had borrowed* it.

34 I (*like*) (*ask*) a question but I was so far back that I didn't think I'd be heard.

35 There (*be*) a fort here at one time. You can see where the foundations were.

36 The dinosaur (*be said*) (*be*) rather a stupid animal.

52 The gerund

C PEG 257

Put the verbs in brackets into the gerund.

1 He gave up (gamble).
2 Try to avoid (make) him angry.
3 Stop (argue) and start (work).
4 The children prefer (watch) TV to (read).
5 I am against (make) any complaints.
6 It's no use (cry) over spilt milk. (*proverb*)
7 I suggest (hold) another meeting next week.
8 He finished (speak) and sat down.
9 He was fined for (drive) without lights.
10 It is difficult to get used to (eat) with chopsticks.
11 If you can't turn the key try (put) some oil in the lock.
12 He lost no time in (get) down to work.
13 You can't make an omelette without (break) eggs. (*proverb*)
14 We are looking forward to (read) your new book.
15 They escaped by (slide) down ropes made of blankets.
16 They don't allow (smoke) in here.
17 He is thinking of (leave) his job and (go) to America.

18 After (read) this article you will give up (smoke).
19 If you put your money into that business you risk (lose) every penny.
20 Imagine (live) with someone who never stops (talk).
21 Is there anything here worth (buy)?
22 He was accused of (steal) official documents and (sell) them.
23 You'd better consult your lawyer before (decide) to buy the property.
24 I don't enjoy (go) to the dentist.
25 Would you mind (put) your pet snake somewhere else?
26 The hostages were rescued without a shot (be) fired.
27 By (work) day and night he succeeded in (finish) the job in time.
28 He has a scheme for (make) grass grow in winter.
29 I don't feel like (work); what about (go) to a disco instead?
30 Would you mind (write) your name and address on the back of the cheque?
31 If a thing is worth (do) at all it is worth (do) well. (*proverb*)
32 I hate (borrow) money.
33 He was furious at (be) mistaken for an escaped convict.
34 After (talk) for ten minutes I succeeded in (convince) him that there was no danger.
35 I remember (read) a review of that book and (think) I'd like to get it.
36 As a result of (listen) at keyholes he learnt many facts which he had no hesitation in (use) to his own advantage.

53 Gerund and infinitive

B PEG 267–71

Put the verbs in brackets into the correct form (gerund or infinitive).

1 I am looking forward to (see) you.
2 He dreads (have) to retire.
3 I arranged (meet) them here.
4 He urged us (work) faster.
5 I wish (see) the manager.
6 It's no use (wait).
7 He warned her (not touch) the wire.
8 Don't forget (lock) the door before (go) to bed.
9 My mother told me (not speak) to anyone about it.
10 I can't understand her (behave) like that.
11 He tried (explain) but she refused (listen).
12 At dinner she annoyed me by (smoke) between the courses.

13 You are expected (know) the safety regulations of the college.
14 He decided (disguise) himself by (dress) as a woman.
15 I am prepared (wait) here all night if necessary.
16 Would you mind (show) me how (work) the lift?
17 After (walk) for three hours we stopped to let the others (catch up) with us.
18 I am beginning (understand) what you mean.
19 He was fined for (exceed) the speed limit.
20 The boys like (play) games but hate (do) lessons.
21 I regret (inform) you that your application has been refused.
22 I couldn't help (overhear) what you said.
23 Mrs Jones: I don't allow (smoke) in my drawing-room.
Mrs Smith: I don't allow my family (smoke) at all.
24 He surprised us all by (go) away without (say) 'Good-bye'.
25 Please go on (write); I don't mind (wait).
26 He wore dark glasses (avoid) (be) recognized.
27 Before (give) evidence you must swear (speak) the truth.
28 I tried (persuade) him (agree) with your proposal.
29 Your windows need (clean); would you like me (do) them for you?
30 Would you mind (shut) the window? I hate (sit) in a draught.
31 I can't help (sneeze); I caught a cold yesterday from (sit) in a draught.
32 Do stop (talk); I am trying (finish) a letter.
33 His doctor advised him (give up) (smoke).
34 My watch keeps (stop).
That's because you keep (forget) (wind) it.
35 Without (realize) it, he hindered us instead of (help) us.
36 People used (make) fire by (rub) two sticks together.

54 Gerund and infinitive

B PEG 267–71

Put the verbs in brackets into the correct form (gerund or infinitive).

1 He hates (answer) the phone, and very often just lets it (ring).
2 If you go on (let) your dog (chase) cars he'll end by (be) run over.
3 I prefer (drive) to (be driven).
4 I advise you (start) (look) for a flat at once.
5 Would you mind (lend) me ten pence? I want (make) a phone call.
6 (Lie) on this beach is much more pleasant than (sit) in the office.
7 She likes her children (go) to a dentist every six months.

8 By (neglect) (take) ordinary precautions he endangered the life of his crew.
9 An instructor is coming (show) us how (use) the aqualung.
10 I have no intention of (go) to that film; I couldn't bear (see) my favourite actress in such a dreadful part.
11 I suggest (telephone) the hospitals before (ask) the police (look) for him.
12 After (hear) the conditions I decided (not enter) for the competition.
13 Some people seem (have) a passion for (write) to the newspapers.
14 He expects me (answer) by return but I have no intention of (reply) at all.
15 I tried (pacify) him but he refused (be pacified) and went on (grumble).
16 By (offer) enormous wages he is persuading men (leave) their present jobs and (work) for him.
17 He postponed (make) a decision till it was too late (do) anything.
18 Imagine (have) (get up) at five a.m. every day!
19 Try (forget) it; it isn't worth (worry) about.
20 There is no point in (remain) in a dangerous place if you can't do anything (help) the people who have (stay) there.
21 The horse won't be well enough (run) in tomorrow's race. He doesn't seem (have recovered) from his long journey.
22 At first I enjoyed (listen) to him but after a while I got tired of (hear) the same story again and again.
23 It is usually easier (learn) a subject by (read) books than by (listen) to lectures.
24 It wouldn't be safe (start) down now; we'll have (wait) till the mist clears.
25 After (discuss) the matter for an hour the committee adjourned without (have reached) any decision.
26 It's not much use (have) a bicycle if you don't know how (ride) it.
27 He didn't dare (leave) the house because he was afraid of (meet) someone who might (recognize) him.
28 I distinctly remember (pay) him. I gave him £2.
29 Did you remember (give) him the key of the safe?
No, I didn't. I'll go and do it now.
30 Please forgive me for (interrupt) you but would you mind (repeat) that last sentence?
31 I know my hair wants (cut) but I never have time (go) to the hairdresser's.
32 He made a lot of money by (buy) tickets in advance and (sell) them

for twice the price on the day of the match.

33 She rushed out of the room without (give) me a chance (explain).

34 He keeps (ask) me the time and I keep (tell) him (buy) himself a watch.

35 He has a theory that it is possible (tell) the time in daylight by (look) into a cat's eyes.

36 I'd hate (be) beside a volcano when it started (erupt).

55 Gerund and infinitive

A PEG 267–71

After **like** it is sometimes possible to use either gerund or infinitive, but there tends to be a slight difference in implication.

like + gerund a usually means 'enjoy';
b usually implies that the action is/was performed;

e.g. *I like skating* = *I enjoy skating* (and do skate).

like + infinitive a has more the meaning of 'approve of', 'like the idea or habit';
b in the affirmative gives no indication as to whether the action is performed or not and in the negative implies that it is not performed.

e.g. *I didn't like saying it* usually means 'I said it, unwillingly', but *I didn't like to say it* usually means 'I didn't say it' (because it didn't seem right or sensible).

The distinction, however, is not rigid. The above notes are, therefore, only guides which may safely be followed.

Put the verbs in brackets into gerund or infinitive.

1 I used (ride) a lot but I haven't had a chance (do) any since (come) here.
I ride sometimes. Would you like (come) with me next time?

2 Most people prefer (spend) money to (earn) it.

3 I resented (be) unjustly accused and asked him (apologize).

4 It isn't good for children (eat) too many sweets.

5 I didn't feel like (work) so I suggested (spend) the day in the garden.

6 Why do you keep (look) back? Are you afraid of (be) followed?

7 Do you remember (post) the letter?
Yes, I remember quite clearly; I posted it in the letter-box near my gate.

8 Did you remember (lock) the door?
No, I didn't. I'd better (go) back and (do) it now.
9 You still have a lot (learn) if you'll forgive my (say) so.
10 It's no use (try) (interrupt) him. You'll have (wait) till he stops (talk).
11 I'm for (do) nothing till the police arrive. They don't like you (move) anything when a crime has been committed.
12 He didn't like (leave) the children alone in the house but he had no alternative as he had (go) out to work.
13 Why didn't you drink it?
I didn't like (drink) it as I didn't know what it was.
14 I'm very sorry for (be) late. It was good of you (wait) for me.
15 I keep (try) (make) mayonnaise but I never succeed.
Try (add) the yolk of a hard-boiled egg.
16 Do you feel like (go) to a film or would you rather (stay) at home?
17 She told me (look) through her correspondence and (take) out any letters that you had written her. I didn't like (look) through someone else's letters but I had (do) as she said.
18 He took to (get up) early and (walk) noisily about the house.
19 I liked (listen) to folk music much better than (listen) to pop.
20 The car began (make) an extraordinary noise so I stopped (see) what it was.
21 You'll never regret (do) a kind action.
22 He decided (put) broken glass on top of his wall (prevent) boys (climb) over it.
23 He annoyed me very much by (take) the piece of cake that I was keeping (eat) after my supper.
24 He kept (ring) up and (ask) for an explanation and she didn't know what (do) about him.
25 We got tired of (wait) for the weather (clear) and finally decided (set) out in the rain.
26 He made me (repeat) his instructions (make) sure that I understood what I was (do) after he had gone.
27 I suggest (leave) the car here and (send) a breakdown van (tow) it to the garage.
28 She apologized for (borrow) my sewing-machine without (ask) permission and promised never (do) it again.
29 I didn't mean (offend) anyone but somehow I succeeded in (annoy) them all.
30 She claimed (be able) (tell) the future by (gaze) into her crystal ball.
31 He never thinks of (get) out of your way; he expects you (walk) round him.

32 You don't need (ask) his permission every time you want (leave) the room.
33 The police accused him of (set) fire to the building but he denied (have been) in the area on the night of the fire.
34 I left my door open. Why didn't you walk in?
I didn't like (go) in when you weren't there.
35 It's much better (go) to a hairdresser than (try) (save) time by (cut) your own hair.
36 I'd rather (earn) my living by (scrub) floors than (make) money by (blackmail) people.

56 Infinitive, gerund, and present participle

A PEG 267–76

This exercise includes examples of both **ing** forms, the gerund and the present participle. Either present participle or infinitive without **to** can be used after verbs of the senses.

Put the verbs in brackets into a correct form. When more than one form is possible it will be noted in the key.

1 When the painter felt the ladder (begin) (slip) he grabbed the gutter (save) himself from (fall).
2 The snow kept (fall) and the workmen grew tired of (try) (keep) the roads clear.
3 He offered (lend) me the money. I didn't like (take) it but I had no alternative.
4 What was in the letter?
I don't know. I didn't like (open) it as it wasn't addressed to me.
5 Do you remember (hear) the bombs (drop)?
No, in the last war I was too young (realize) what was happening.
6 Did you remember (book) seats for the theatre tomorrow?
Yes, I have the tickets here. Would you like (keep) them? I am inclined (lose) theatre tickets.
7 Try (avoid) (be) late. He hates (be) kept (wait).
8 I didn't know how (get) to your house so I stopped (ask) the way.
9 I wish my refrigerator would stop (make) that horrible noise. You can't hear anyone (speak).
10 This book tells you how (win) at games without actually (cheat).
11 The enemy began (fire). He felt bullets (strike) the wall behind him.

12 He heard the clock (strike) six and knew that it was time for him (get) up.
13 I can hear the bell (ring) but nobody seems (be coming) (open) the door.
14 Did you advise him (go) to the police?
No, I didn't like (give) any advice on such a difficult matter.
15 He wanted (put) my chameleon on a tartan rug and (watch) it (change) colour.
16 It is easy (see) animals on the road in daylight but sometimes at night it is very difficult (avoid) (hit) them.
17 The fire seems (be) out.
It can't be quite out. I can hear the wood (crackle).
18 I caught him (climb) over my wall. I asked him (explain) but he refused (say) anything, so in the end I had (let) him (go).
19 When at last I succeeded in (convince) him that I wanted (get) home quickly he put his foot on the accelerator and I felt the car (leap) forward.
20 I'm not used to (drive) on the left.
When you see everyone else (do) it you'll find it quite easy (do) yourself.
21 It is pleasant (sit) by the fire at night and (hear) the wind (howl) outside.
22 There was no way of (get) out of the building except by (climb) down a rope and Ann was too terrified (do) this.
23 We heard the engines (roar) as the plane began (move) and we saw the people on the ground (wave) good-bye.
24 It's no good (write) to him; he never answer letters. The only thing (do) is (go) and (see) him.
25 Why did you go all round the field instead of (walk) across it?
I didn't like (cross) it because of the bull. I never see a bull without (think) that it wants (chase) me.
26 The people in the flat below seem (be having) a party. You can hear the champagne corks (thud) against their ceiling.
27 I don't like (get) bills but when I do get them I like (pay) them promptly.
28 Ask him (come) in. Don't keep him (stand) at the door.
29 The boys next door used (like) (make) and (fly) model aeroplanes, but they seem to have stopped (do) that now.
30 I knew I wasn't the first (arrive), for I saw smoke (rise) from the chimney.
31 We watched the men (saw) the tree and as we were walking away heard it (fall) with a tremendous crash.

32 I hate (see) a child (cry).
33 We watched the children (jump) from a window and (fall) into a blanket held by the people below.
34 It is very unpleasant (wake) up and (hear) the rain (beat) on the windows.
35 He saw the lorry (begin) (roll) forwards but he was too far away (do) anything (stop) it.
36 There are people who can't help (laugh) when they see someone (slip) on a banana skin.

57 Using participles to join sentences

B PEG 275–6

Join each of the following pairs of sentences, using either a present participle e.g. *knowing*, a past participle e.g. *known*, or a perfect participle e.g. *having known*. Numbers 17, 28, 33, and 36 contain three sentences each. Combine these in the same way.

These participle constructions are more common in written English.

e.g. He got off his horse. He began searching for something on the ground.
Getting off his horse, he began searching . . .
I had seen photographs of the place, I had no desire to go there.
Having seen photographs of the place, I had no desire . . .
The speaker refused to continue. He was infuriated by the interruptions.
Infuriated by the interruptions, the speaker refused . . .

1 I knew that he was poor. I offered to pay his fare.
2 We barricaded the windows. We assembled in the hall.
3 She became tired of my complaints about the programme. She turned it off.
4 He found no one at home. He left the house in a bad temper.
5 She hoped to find the will. She searched everywhere.
6 The criminal removed all traces of his crime. He left the building.
7 He realized that he had missed the last train. He began to walk.
8 He was exhausted by his work. He threw himself on his bed.
9 He had spent all his money. He decided to go home and ask his father for a job.
10 He escaped from prison. He looked for a place where he could get food.

11 She didn't want to hear the story again. She had heard it all before.
12 They found the treasure. They began quarrelling about how to divide it.
13 She entered the room suddenly. She found them smoking.
14 I turned on the light. I was astonished at what I saw.
15 We visited the museum. We decided to have lunch in the park.
16 He offered to show us the way home. He thought we were lost.
17 He found his revolver. He loaded it. He sat down facing the door.
18 She asked me to help her. She realized that she couldn't move it alone.
19 He fed the dog. He sat down to his own dinner.
20 He addressed the congregation. He said he was sorry to see how few of them had been able to come.
21 He thought he must have made a mistake somewhere. He went through his calculations again.
22 I have looked through the fashion magazines. I realize that my clothes are hopelessly out of date.
23 The tree had fallen across the road. It had been uprooted by the gale.
24 People were sleeping in the next room. They were wakened by the sound of breaking glass.
25 I knew that the murderer was still at large. I was extremely reluctant to open the door.
26 He stole the silver. He looked for a place to hide it.
27 We were soaked to the skin. We eventually reached the station.
28 I sat in the front row. I used a pair of binoculars. I saw everything beautifully.
29 One day you will be sitting by the fire. You will take down this book.
30 I didn't like to sit down. I knew that there were ants in the grass.
31 She believed that she could trust him absolutely. She gave him a blank cheque.
32 Slates were ripped off by the gale. They fell on people passing below.
33 The lion found his cage door open. He saw no sign of his keeper. He left the cage and walked slowly towards the zoo entrance.
34 The government once tried to tax people according to the size of their houses. They put a tax on windows.
35 I had heard that the caves were dangerous. I didn't like to go any further without a light.
36 She wore extremely fashionable clothes. She was surrounded by photographers and pressmen. She swept up to the microphone.

58 Misrelated participles

A PEG 279

A participle is considered to belong to the noun or pronoun that immediately precedes it (which usually, but not necessarily, is the subject of the main verb).

e.g. *The boy,* climbing *the tree to get birds' eggs, had a bad fall.*

If there is no noun/pronoun in this position the participle is considered to belong to the subject of the following main verb:

Climbing *the tree to get birds' eggs, the boy had a bad fall.*

Sometimes this principle is disregarded and confusion results:

e.g. *Climbing down the tree, one of the eggs broke.*

This word order makes it appear that the egg was climbing, which is nonsense. A participle linked in this way to the wrong noun/pronoun is said to be 'misrelated'. The sentence should be rewritten:

Climbing down the tree he broke one of the eggs
or *As he was climbing down the tree one of the eggs broke.*

Other examples of this type of error are given below. Correct the sentences.

1 When leaving a car in this car park the brakes must be left off.
2 Wading across the river, the current swept me off my feet.
3 When filling a tank with petrol naked lights should be extinguished.
4 Running into the room, a rug caught her foot and she fell.
5 Reading the letter a second time, the meaning becomes clearer.
6 When carrying a gun it should never be pointed at anyone.
7 When planting these flowers care must be taken not to damage the roots.
8 Riding in his first race, his horse fell at the last jump.
9 When paying by cheque, the cheque should be crossed 'and Co.'.
10 Knowing me to be the fool of the family, the news that I had won a scholarship astonished him.
11 Believing that his last hour had come, his hands began to tremble.
12 Passing under a ladder, a pot of paint fell on my head.
13 Reading in bed, my hands often get very cold.
14 Leaving the cinema, it seemed to him that the film had been exceptionally bad.

15 Barking furiously, I led the dog out of the room.
16 Having paid my taxes, the amount left in the bank is hardly worth mentioning.
17 Writing my name in the hotel register, a familiar voice attracted my attention.
18 Tied to a post, the sea was tossing the boat up and down.
19 Misunderstanding the question, the wrong answer was sent in.
20 Shining in the sky, we saw the first star.
21 When driving carelessly it is easy to have an accident.
22 Pinned to the door by a knife, the men saw a notice.
23 Written in large letters they read the words 'No Entry'.
24 While cleaning his gun it went off unexpectedly.
25 Wondering where to go, an advertisement caught her eye.
26 Rushing out of the house, a lorry knocked me over.
27 Sitting by the fire, it all comes back to me.
28 Falling from such a height, we thought he would never survive.
29 When changing a fuse the electricity should first be switched off.
30 Towed behind the car, I saw a trailer with a boat on it.
31 While sitting at the foot of a cliff a stone fell on him.
32 Uprooted by the gale, the road was blocked by a huge tree.
33 Dropped by parachute, the country seemed entirely unfamiliar.
34 Sitting in the dentist's chair, an idea suddenly occurred to me.
35 Weakened by his last illness, I felt sure that another winter in this country would kill him.
36 Getting out of bed, a scorpion bit him.

4 Auxiliary verbs

59 Auxiliary verbs, negative and interrogative

C PEG 102–3

Make these sentences (a) negative and (b) interrogative, following the usual rule for auxiliary verbs. (Auxiliaries are used here both by themselves and as part of various tenses of ordinary verbs.)

1 They can read French.
2 He is ten years old.
3 He may use this one.
4 They have two cars.
5 She was furious.
6 He should try again.
7 It could be done.
8 You were right.
9 You must tell him.
10 He can leave it here.
11 It will fit in his pocket.
12 She has a headache.
13 I shall be here.
14 She is afraid of mice.
15 She may borrow the car.
16 He is sorry for her.
17 There will be a lot to do.
18 He'll recognize her.
19 I have seen you before.
20 He'll be able to carry it.
21 It's very hot.
22 They used to live here.
23 The river was four metres deep.
24 We must hurry. (Use **needn't** in the negative.)
25 He ought to wait.
26 He would enjoy it.
27 They are having lunch.
28 We have finished.

29 You are hungry.
30 He can do without cigarettes.
31 She'll wait for you.
32 He used to eat them raw.
33 There'll be plenty for everyone.
34 He was very bad-tempered.
35 She is leaving tonight.
36 You are very good at this.

60 Auxiliaries and ordinary verbs, negative and interrogative

C PEG 96, 99–100, 102–3

Some auxiliaries when used in certain ways make their negative and interrogative according to the rule for ordinary verbs, i.e. with **do**. The verbs in the following examples are either auxiliaries used in these ways, or ordinary verbs.

Make the sentences (a) negative and (b) interrogative, using **do**.

1 They have eggs for breakfast.
2 He needs a new coat.
3 Your cat catches mice.
4 They have to work hard.
5 She does the housework.
6 We know the place.
7 You like mushrooms.
8 He understood me.
9 He needs more money.
10 You drink coffee.
11 He had to borrow one.
12 The journey takes two hours.
13 He made a lot of mistakes.
14 She had a look at it.
15 Her hair needed cutting.
16 It matters very much.
17 He does his homework after supper.
18 She has a cold bath every morning.
19 They like a lot of noise.
20 She had to make a speech.
21 He does his best.

22 He has to get up at six every day.
23 You have lunch at one.
24 He uses an axe.
25 She dared him to climb it.
26 You did it on purpose.
27 He has his house painted every year.
28 He dared to say that!
29 They had a good time.
30 The drink did him good.
31 My watch wants cleaning.
32 She came again.
33 He had to wait for you.
34 You had your house painted.
35 They went by bus.
36 They buy ices.

61 *have*, possessive

B PEG 119

In British English, **have** meaning **possess** is not normally conjugated with **do** except when there is an idea of habit.

e.g. *I haven't* (*got*) a watch.	(present possession)
How many corners *has* a cube?	(a characteristic rather than a habit)
He *doesn't* usually *have* time to study.	(habit)

In the past, **did** is used for habit; otherwise either form is possible:

e.g. *Did you have/had you* an umbrella when you left the house?

In other English-speaking countries, however, the **do** forms are used almost exclusively. It would therefore be possible to use **do/did** forms throughout the following exercises (except in No. 27), but students are asked to use **have not/have you** forms where they could be used. Where both are equally usual this will be noted in the key.

Fill the spaces with the correct forms of **have**, adding **got** where possible. Only one space will be left in each clause, but note that **got** may be separated from **have** by another word. When a negative form is required '(negative)' will be placed at the end of the example.

1 He is standing there in the rain and . . . even the sense to put up his umbrella. (negative)
2 He . . . a cold in the head.
That's nothing new; he always . . . a cold.
3 I . . . brainwaves very often, but I . . . one now. (1st verb negative)
4 It is no good arguing with someone who . . . a bee in his bonnet.
5 Why don't you say something? You . . . an excuse? (negative)
6 You . . . this toothache yesterday?
7 How many letters . . . the alphabet?
8 The houses in your country . . . flat roofs?
9 You . . . the time? (= do you know the time)
No, I . . . a watch. (negative)
10 You ever . . . an impulse to smash something?
11 He . . . £1,000 a year when his father dies.
12 Air passengers usually . . . much luggage. (negative)
13 You . . . any objection to sitting with your back to the engine?
14 Oysters . . . always pearls in them. (negative)
15 Your door . . . a little hole through which you can peep at callers? (negative)
16 You . . . a match on you?
No, I don't smoke so I never . . . matches.
17 What is your opinion?
I . . . an opinion. (negative)
18 That cup . . . a crack in it.
19 You . . . any suspicion who did it?
20 This desk . . . a secret drawer?
No, modern desks ever . . . secret drawers. (negative)
21 When you go to a place for the first time, you ever . . . a feeling that you've been there before?
22 Babies . . . teeth when they're born?
23 How many sides . . . a pentagon?
24 Our cat . . . kittens every year.
How many she . . . each time?
25 They say that if children . . . complete freedom when they are young, they . . . inhibitions when they grow up. (2nd verb negative)
26 You . . . mosquitoes in your country in summer?
27 You . . . children?
Yes, I . . . two, a boy and a girl.
28 You . . . a motor cycle?
No, I only . . . an ordinary bicycle, but I . . . a motor cycle next year.
29 Why do you suddenly want to back out? You . . . cold feet?

30 Customer: You . . . any mushrooms today?
Shopkeeper: We usually . . . them but I'm afraid we . . . any at the moment. (last verb negative)
31 I think I know the man you mean. He . . . one blue eye and one brown one? (negative)
32 Children nowadays . . . far too much pocket money. I . . . any when I was at school. (2nd verb negative)
33 We were always getting lost in the desert.
You . . . compasses? (negative)
34 Red-haired people always . . . bad tempers?
35 Do you think we should eat this meat? It . . . a very nice smell. (negative)
36 The stairs are on fire! You . . . a long rope?

62 *have*, various uses

B PEG 120

have can mean **take** (a meal/lesson/bath, etc.), **entertain** (guests), **encounter** (difficulty, etc.), **enjoy** (a time/journey, etc.). When used in these ways

1 **have** usually forms its negative and interrogative with **do**.
2 **have** can be used in the continuous tenses.

Put the correct form of **have** into the following sentences. Use **am having, is having**, etc., as a future form.

1 We . . . some friends in for dinner tomorrow night.
2 You . . . a good journey yesterday?
3 Don't disturb him; he . . . a rest.
4 We . . . lunch early tomorrow.
5 How many lessons he . . . a week?
He usually . . . four.
6 You . . . earthquakes in your country?
7 What time you . . . breakfast?
We usually . . . it at 8.00.
8 What you . . . for breakfast?
We . . . toast and coffee.
9 Why you . . . a cooked breakfast? (negative)
It's too much trouble.
10 Why were they making such a noise?
They . . . an argument.

11 You . . . a thunderstorm yesterday?
12 Come in, we . . . a debate.
13 You . . . a cup of coffee?
Yes, please.
14 You're wanted on the phone.
I can't come, I . . . a bath.
15 The tree just missed the roof, we . . . a very lucky escape.
16 How did you damage your car? You . . . an accident?
17 I . . . a look at that house tomorrow. If I like it I'll buy it.
18 We . . . very bad weather just now.
19 I . . . a very interesting conversation with the milkman when my neighbour interrupted me.
20 English people always . . . roast beef for lunch on Sundays?
21 It is difficult to learn a foreign language when you . . . an opportunity of speaking it. (negative)
22 The farmers . . . a lot of trouble with foxes at present.
23 On the whole women drivers . . . so many accidents as men drivers. (negative)
24 You . . . anything to eat before you left home?
Oh yes, I . . . bacon and eggs.
25 You . . . any difficulty getting into your flat last night?
26 Are you enjoying yourself?
Yes, I . . . a wonderful time.
27 How often he . . . a bath?
28 You . . . a good night?
No, I slept very badly.
29 Why were they late?
They . . . a puncture.
30 We . . . a party here next week. Would you like to come?
31 Why didn't you speak to her?
I . . . a chance. (negative)
32 We . . . a lecture next Monday.
33 I . . . tea with her tomorrow.
34 He . . . an operation next week.
35 He ever . . . nightmares?
36 When he got tired of it I . . . a try.
You . . . any luck?
Yes, I caught a great big fish.

63 The *have* + object + past participle construction

B PEG 117

Part 1 Fill in the spaces by inserting the correct form of **have**. Use **am/is/are having** as a future form. (**get** can be used instead of **have**, but is more colloquial.)

1 I . . . my house painted. That is why there is all this mess.
2 I know my hair looks dreadful but I . . . it set tomorrow.
3 The hall was dark so last year we . . . another window put in.
4 That dead tree is dangerous. I . . . it cut down tomorrow.
5 The house was damp so last winter we . . . central heating installed.
6 I can't read Greek so I . . . the documents translated. My nephew is helping with the translation.
7 Our swimming pool is too small so we . . . a new one made. They are starting work on it next week.
8 Why he . . . all his shoes specially made?
He says that he has to because his feet are different sizes.
9 You . . . your milk delivered or do you go to the shop for it?
10 If you hate cleaning fish why you . . . them cleaned at the fishmonger's? (negative)
11 How often you . . . your dog clipped?
12 I'm afraid it's rather draughty here but I . . . that broken pane replaced tomorrow.

Part 2 Fill in the spaces by inserting the correct form of **have**, the past participle of the verb in brackets and, where necessary, a pronoun.

13 We must . . . the grass . . . It is far too long. (cut)
14 Your roof is leaking, you should . . . it . . . (repair)
15 My skirt is too long, I must . . . (shorten)
16 No one will be able to read your notes.
I know; I . . . them . . . (type)
17 That's a good piano but you should . . . it . . . (tune)
18 I've got paint on my coat; now I'll have to . . . (clean)
19 He didn't like the colour of the curtains so he . . . (dye)
20 He went to a garage to . . . the puncture . . . (mend)
21 His arm was broken so he went to hospital to . . . (set)
22 That tooth is giving you a lot of trouble; you should . . . (take out)
23 The room is very shabby; but I . . . next month. (redecorate)
24 They couldn't find a house to suit them so they . . . one . . . (build)

Part 3 Rewrite the sentences using a **have** + object + past participle construction and omitting the words underlined.

e.g. *I employed a plumber to examine my boiler* would be rewritten:
I had my boiler examined.

25 I pay a garage to grease my car.
26 The tap kept dripping so I sent for a plumber to see to it.
27 I paid a watchmaker to clean my watch.
28 The shoe-mender is repairing my shoes for me.
29 They arranged for the police to arrest the man.
30 He paid a lorry driver to tow the car to a garage.
31 They employed builders to put a new roof on the house.
32 I pay a window cleaner to clean my windows every month.
33 I went to an oculist and he tested my eyes for me.
34 I can't buy clothes to fit me so I employ a tailor to make them for me.
35 I asked the fishmonger to open the oysters for me.
36 I went to a jeweller and he pierced my ears for me.

64 *be*

A PEG 109–14, 219, 286–7, 302

This is a general exercise which includes infinitives, subjunctives, conditionals, and some examples of the **be** + infinitive construction. When this last construction or a passive construction is required the second verb is given in brackets at the end of the sentence.

e.g. Why are all those dogs wearing harness?
They . . . as guide dogs for the blind. (train)
They are being trained as guide dogs for the blind.

Fill the spaces in the following sentences by inserting the correct form of **be** with, where necessary, the past participle or present or perfect infinitive of the verb in brackets.

Remember that, in the passive, **be** can be used in the continuous tenses.

1 They are cutting down all the trees. The countryside . . . (ruin)
2 The Prime Minister . . . a speech tonight. I think we should listen to it. (make)
3 If I . . . you I'd go on to the next exercise.
4 . . . late once is excusable but . . . late every day is not.
5 He ordered that all lights . . . (extinguish)

6 How long you . . . waiting?
7 My flat was full of dust because the old house just opposite . . . (pull down)
8 He asked where he . . . it. (put)
I told him to put it on the mantelpiece.
9 It . . . difficult to read a newspaper upside down? (use neg.)
10 You . . . here till I return. That is an order. (stay)
11 He suggests that prominent people . . . to contribute. (ask)
12 Even if you . . . to go on your knees to him I don't think it would make him change his mind.
13 I . . . on a catering course when I leave school. My parents have arranged it. (go)
14 What is happening now?
The injured man . . . out of the arena. (carry)
15 It's better . . . too early than too late.
16 I wish you . . . here. I miss you very much.
17 Why did you leave him behind? You . . . him with you. (Those were your instructions.) (take)
18 She is learning Italian. She . . . by a professor from Milan. (teach)
19 I know I . . . half an hour late yesterday but I . . . half an hour early tomorrow.
I'd rather you . . . punctual every day.
20 It is impossible . . . right every time.
21 He . . . here by seven but now it's nine and there's no sign of him. (be)
22 They decided that voting papers . . . to all members. (send)
23 There . . . eggs for breakfast tomorrow?
24 If only I . . . there! (but I wasn't.)
25 The Queen . . . the new hospital next week. (open)
26 I couldn't see the man who was leading us and I didn't know where we . . . (take)
27 It . . . a trilogy but in the end the author found that he had only enough material for two volumes. (be)
28 You . . . very angry if I refused?
29 The matter . . . discussed in tomorrow's debate.
30 His mare . . . in tomorrow's race but he said this morning that she was sick and wouldn't be running after all. (run)
31 The house wasn't ready; it still . . . and there were pots of paint and ladders everywhere. (paint)
32 They decided that an expurgated edition . . . for use in schools. (print)

33 His works are immensely popular; they . . . into all the major European languages. (translate)
34 It is high time you . . . in bed.
35 I had my instructions and I knew exactly what I . . . (do)
36 If this report . . . believed, we are going to have a very severe drought.

65 *can* and *be able*

B PEG 130–3, 215 B, 216 B, 217 B, 309

Part 1 **can**, used to express ability with **could, shall/will be able**

Fill the following spaces, using **can** for present, **could** for past and **shall/will be able** for future. There is no need to use other **able** forms in this section. Put **to** where necessary before the infinitives.

1 . . . you stand on your head?
I . . . when I was at school but I . . . now. (second verb neg.)
2 When I've passed my driving test I . . . hire a car from our local garage.
3 At the end of the month the Post Office will send him an enormous telephone bill which he . . . pay. (neg.)
4 I . . . remember the address. (neg.)
. . . you even remember the street? (neg.)
5 When the fog lifts we . . . see where we are.
6 You've put too much in your rucksack; you never . . . carry all that.
7 When I was a child I . . . understand adults, and now that I am an adult I . . . understand children. (neg., neg.)
8 When you have taken your degree you . . . put B.A. after your name?
9 Don't try to look at all the pictures in the gallery. Otherwise when you get home you . . . remember any of them. (neg.)
10 When I first went to Spain I . . . read Spanish but I . . . speak it. (second verb neg.)
11 . . . you type?
Yes, I . . . type but I . . . do shorthand. (second verb neg.)
12 I'm locked in. I . . . get out! (neg.)
. . . you squeeze between the bars? (neg.)
No! I . . .; I'm too fat. (neg.)

Part 2 **could** and **was able**

In some of the following sentences either **could** or **was able** could be used. In others only **was/were able** is possible. Fill the spaces and put **to** where necessary before the infinitives.

13 He was very strong; he . . . ski all day and dance all night.
14 The car plunged into the river. The driver . . . get out but the passengers were drowned.
15 I was a long way from the stage. I . . . see all right but I . . . hear very well. (second verb neg.)
16 We . . . borrow umbrellas; so we didn't get wet.
17 . . . you walk or did they have to carry you?
18 I had no key so I . . . lock the door. (neg.)
19 I knew the town so I . . . advise him where to go.
20 When the garage had repaired our car we . . . continue our journey.
21 At five years old he . . . read quite well.
22 When I arrived everyone was asleep. Fortunately I . . . wake my sister and she let me in.
23 The swimmer was very tired but he . . . reach the shore before he collapsed.
24 The police were suspicious at first but I . . . convince them that we were innocent.

Part 3

This section includes examples of **could** used for polite requests and as a conditional.

25 . . . I speak to Mr Pitt, please?
I'm afraid he's out at the moment. . . . you ring back later?
26 If you stood on my shoulders . . . you reach the top of the wall?
No, I'm afraid I . . . (neg.)
27 If I sang . . . you accompany me on the piano?
No, I . . .; I . . . play the piano! (neg., neg.)
28 If a letter comes for me . . . you please forward it to this address?
29 She made the wall very high so that boys . . . climb over it. (neg.)
30 They took his passport so that he . . . leave the country. (neg.)
31 . . . you tell me the time, please?
I'm afraid I. . . . I haven't got a watch. (neg.)
32 If you had to, . . . you go without food for a week?
I suppose I . . . if I had plenty of water.

33 . . . you lend me £5?
No, I . . . (neg.)
34 They used to chain valuable books to library desks so that people . . . take them away. (neg.)
35 He says that he saw Clementine drowning but . . . help her as he . . . swim. (neg., neg.)
36 If you had had the right tools . . . you have repaired the engine?

66 *may*

C PEG 124–7, 215 B, 216 B, 217 B, 309

Fill the spaces by inserting the correct form of **may**.

1 It . . . rain, you'd better take a coat.
2 He said that it . . . rain.
3 We . . . as well stay here till the weather improves.
4 . . . I borrow your umbrella?
5 You . . . tell me! (I think I have a right to know.)
6 Candidates . . . not bring textbooks into the examination room.
7 If we wave to him he . . . give us a lift.
8 If he knew our address he . . . come and see us.
9 . . . I come in?
Please do.
10 We must all work hard so that our country . . . be prosperous.
11 I think I left my glasses in your office. You . . . ask your secretary to look for them for me.
12 . . . all your wishes come true!
13 I . . . never see you again.
14 He . . . be on the next train. We . . . as well wait.
15 If we got there early we . . . get a good seat.
16 . . . I give you some advice?
If you must.
17 You ought to buy now; prices . . . go up.
18 I'll wait a week so that he . . . have time to think it over.
19 He isn't going to eat it; I . . . as well give it to the dog.
20 They sacrificed their lives so that we . . . live.
21 You . . . have written. (I am annoyed/disappointed that you didn't.)
22 We'd better be early; there . . . be a crowd.
23 Nobody knows how people first came to these islands. They . . . have sailed from South America on rafts.

24 I can't think what to do.
. . . I make a suggestion?
25 He said that we . . . use his flat whenever we liked.
26 I don't think I'll succeed but I . . . as well try.
27 You ought to go to his lectures, you . . . learn something.
28 If we can give him a blood transfusion we . . . be able to save his life.
29 Two parallel white lines in the middle of the road mean that you . . . not overtake.
30 If I bought a lottery ticket I . . . win £1,000.
31 If you said that, he . . . be very offended.
32 I wonder why they didn't go.
The weather . . . have been too bad.
33 They used to hang criminals in public so that everyone . . . see the reward for crime.
34 He has refused, but he . . . change his mind if you asked him again.
35 . . . I see your passport, please?
36 You . . . be right but I don't think you are.

67 Short answers using auxiliary verbs

C PEG 104

Answer these questions using **yes/no**+ pronoun + an auxiliary.

e.g Did you go? Yes, I did *or*: No, I didn't.
Can you swim? Yes, I can *or*: No, I can't.

1 Are you afraid of mice?
2 Is she at home?
3 Do you know French?
4 Did you see him?
5 Is the lift working?
6 Was Mary angry?
7 Have you had breakfast?
8 Can he cook?
9 Should you say anything?
10 Will you come?
11 Did I tread on your toe?
12 May I go now?
13 Used he to live here?
14 Has she paid the bill?
15 Could you lend it to me?

16 Must you go? (use **needn't** in the negative)
17 Was there a lot to do?
18 Need I say anything? (use **must** in the affirmative)
19 Does he drink whisky?
20 Did you do it on purpose?
21 May I take one?
22 Will you have to pay for it?
23 Has he been there?
24 Would you like to go?
25 Does Ann play cards?
26 Are you doing anything tonight?
27 Was it very difficult?
28 Had he realized this?
29 Were they surprised?
30 Would you like another cup?
31 Do you have to wear glasses?
32 Did your mother say anything?
33 Could he have prevented it?
34 Must he report to the police? (use **needn't** in the negative)
35 Were there mosquitoes?
36 Have you had enough of this?

68 Question tags

C PEG 106

Add question tags to the following sentences.

e.g. He was asleep, *wasn't he?* You can't swim, *can you?*
Ann knew it, *didn't she?* He didn't see it, *did he?*

1 It's cold.
2 Tom has a car.
3 I may take it.
4 You can come.
5 He should drive slowly.
6 You eat oysters.
7 They'll have time.
8 You knew that.
9 He plays well.
10 She used to live here.
11 I was right.

12 He likes it.
13 You won't be long.
14 She didn't find it.
15 They needn't pay.
16 They aren't allowed to play cards.
17 She doesn't know you.
18 I needn't say anything.
19 You won't tell anyone.
20 It isn't expensive.
21 He didn't win.
22 He shouldn't put so much salt in it.
23 We shan't be here.
24 The food wasn't bad.
25 You ought to be there.
26 You heard me.
27 It was struck by lightning.
28 You wouldn't think it.
29 There's a good bus service.
30 He is used to it.
31 You aren't angry?
32 He hasn't been long.
33 He'd rather stay here.
34 We'd better go.
35 You can do without it.
36 He died last year.

69 Additions to remarks, using auxiliary verbs

C PEG 108

Part 1 Add to the following remarks using **(and) so** + the noun/pronoun in brackets + the auxiliary. If there is an auxiliary in the first remark repeat this; if not use **do/does/did**.

e.g. He lives in London. (I) He lives in London *and so do I.*
He had to wait. (you) He had to wait *and so had you.*

1 I have read it. (John)
2 He is a writer. (she)
3 Tom can speak Welsh. (his wife)
4 She ought to get up. (you)
5 He wants to help us. (she)

6 The pork was bad. (the beef)
7 The first bus was full. (the second)
8 I bought a ticket. (my brother)
9 You must come. (your son)
10 This bus goes to Piccadilly. (that)
11 I'm getting out at the next stop. (my friend)
12 He used to work in a restaurant. (I)

Part 2 Add to the following remarks using **(and) neither/nor** + the auxiliary + the noun/pronoun in brackets.

e.g. He isn't back. (she) He isn't back *and neither is she.*

13 I haven't seen it. (Tom)
14 You don't know the way. (your aunt)
15 They didn't use it. (we)
16 He can't come. (his sister)
17 I don't believe it. (Ann)
18 Alice couldn't understand. (Andrew)
19 I'm not going. (you)
20 This telephone doesn't work. (that)
21 Tom's car won't start. (mine)
22 I hadn't any change. (the taxi driver)
23 He didn't know the way. (anyone else)
24 My father wouldn't mind. (my mother)

Part 3 Contrary additions.
Add to the following remarks using **but** + noun/pronoun + the auxiliary or **do/does/did**. Make a negative addition to an affirmative remark:

e.g. She thanked me. (he) She thanked me *but he didn't.*

Make an affirmative addition to a negative remark:

e.g. She can't eat oysters. (I) She can't eat oysters *but I can.*

Use **needn't** as the negative of **must**, and **must** as the affirmative of **needn't**.

25 John was seasick. (Mary)
26 He wasn't there. (she)
27 You must go. (your brother)
28 My sister can speak German. (I)
29 Alexander didn't want to wait. (James)
30 Bill needn't stay. (Stanley)

31 A cat wouldn't eat it. (a dog)
32 He will enjoy it. (his wife)
33 The teacher hadn't got a television set. (his pupils)
34 This beach is safe for bathing. (that beach)
35 I must be there early. (you)
36 Swallows leave England in autumn. (robins)

70 Agreements and disagreements with remarks, using auxiliary verbs

C PEG 105

Part 1 Agreements with affirmative remarks.
Agree with the following remarks, using **yes/so** + pronoun + the auxiliary or **do/does/did**.

e.g. He has a good influence on her. *Yes, he has.*

1 We must have a large room.
2 I was very rude.
3 She always wears dark glasses.
4 She may be a spy.
5 He does his work well.
6 There's a snake in that basket.
7 He needs six bottles.
8 The rain is coming through the roof.
9 His revolver was loaded.
10 He looks dishonest.
11 They used to have a parrot.
12 The fog is getting thicker.

Part 2 Agreements with negative remarks.
Agree with the following remarks, using **no** + pronoun + the auxiliary.

e.g. Elephants never forget. *No, they don't.*

13 Cuckoos don't build nests.
14 He didn't complain.
15 It isn't worth keeping.
16 He can't help coughing.
17 The ice wasn't thick enough.
18 The lift wouldn't come down.
19 This flat hasn't got very thick walls.

20 They don't have earthquakes there.
21 The oranges didn't look very good.
22 It hasn't been a bad summer.
23 I don't look my age.
24 He mightn't like that colour.

Part 3 Disagreements with affirmative or negative remarks.
Disagree with the following remarks, using **oh no/but** + pronoun + auxiliary. Use a negative auxiliary if the first verb is affirmative and an affirmative auxiliary if the first verb is negative.

e.g. He won't be any use. *(Oh) yes, he will.*
She worked here for a year. *(Oh) no, she didn't.*

25 You're drunk.
26 I didn't do it on purpose.
27 They weren't in your way.
28 I wasn't born then.
29 She'd rather live alone.
30 You gave him my address.
31 I can use your bicycle.
32 That five pound note belongs to me.
33 He didn't mean to be rude.
34 Children should be seen and not heard.
35 I know where you went.
36 She promised to obey him.

71 Auxiliaries followed by infinitive with or without *to*

C PEG 103 E

Put **to** where necessary before the infinitives in brackets.

1 You needn't (come) tomorrow.
2 People used (travel) on horseback.
3 I'll have (hurry).
4 You ought (take) a holiday.
5 I'll (lend) him some money.
6 You are (go) at once.
7 We didn't have (pay) anything.

8 There won't (be) enough room for everyone.
9 You can (see) the windmill from here.
10 He was able (explain).
11 We may have (stay) here all night.
12 He used (spend) a lot of time in his library.
13 He didn't dare (say) anything.
14 Don't (move).
15 We'll (look) for a hotel.
16 You needn't (look) for a hotel; I'll be able (put) you up.
17 The doctor said that I ought (give up) smoking.
18 He used (drink) quite a lot.
19 He should (be) ready by now.
20 May I (ask) you a question?
21 I shan't be able (do) it till after the holidays.
22 I didn't need (say) anything.
23 How dare you (open) my letters!
24 They ought (warn) people about the dangerous currents.
25 I should (say) nothing about it if I were you.
26 You are not (mention) this to anyone.
27 Why do they (obey) him? They don't dare (refuse).
28 You must (look) both ways before crossing the road.
29 Your map may (have been) out of date.
30 You ought (have finished) it last night.
31 I must (say) I think you behaved very badly.
32 I shouldn't have (carry) my own luggage.
33 We've got (get out).
34 It might (kill) somebody.
35 I was able (rescue) him.
36 He had (share) a cabin.

72 *must* and *have to*

B PEG 135–45

Fill the spaces in the following sentences by inserting **must** or the present, future, or past form of **have to.**

1 She . . . leave home at eight every morning at present.
2 Notice in a picture gallery: Cameras, sticks and umbrellas . . . be left at the desk.
3 He sees very badly; he . . . wear glasses all the time.
4 I . . . do all the typing at my office.

5 You . . . read this book. It's really excellent.
6 The children . . . play in the streets till their mothers get home from work.
7 She felt ill and . . . leave early.
8 Mr Pitt . . . cook his own meals. His wife is away.
9 I hadn't enough money and I . . . pay by cheque.
10 I never remember his address; I always . . . look it up.
11 Employer: You . . . come to work in time.
12 If you go to a dentist with a private practice you . . . pay him quite a lot of money.
13 Father to small son: You . . . do what Mummy says.
14 My neighbour's child . . . practise the piano for three hours a day.
15 Doctor: I can't come now.
Caller: You . . . come; he's terribly ill.
16 English children . . . stay at school till the age of 16.
17 In my district there is no gas laid on. People . . . use electricity for everything.
18 Notice above petrol pump: All engines . . . be switched off.
19 Mother to daughter: You . . . come in earlier at night.
20 The shops here don't deliver. We . . . carry everything home ourselves.
21 The buses were all full; I . . . get a taxi.
22 Notice beside escalators: Dogs and push chairs . . . be carried.
23 'Au pair' girls usually . . . do quite a lot of housework.
24 Tell her that she . . . be here by six. I insist on it.
25 When a tyre is punctured the driver . . . change the wheel.
26 Park notice: All dogs . . . be kept on leads.
27 She . . . learn how to drive when her local railway station is closed.
28 Railway notice: Passengers . . . cross the line by the footbridge.
29 I got lost and . . . ask a policeman the way.
30 Farmers . . . get up early.
31 If you buy that television set you . . . buy a licence for it.
32 When I changed my job I . . . move to another flat.
33 Waiters . . . pay tax on the tips that they receive.
34 Father to son: I can't support you any longer; you . . . earn your own living from now on.
35 Railway notice: Passengers . . . be in possession of a ticket.
36 Whenever the dog wants to go out I . . . get up and open the door.

73 *must not* and *need not*

C PEG 137

Use **must not** or **need not** to fill the spaces in the following sentences.

1 You . . . ring the bell; I have a key.
2 Notice in cinema: Exit doors . . . be locked during performances.
3 You . . . drink this: it is poison.
4 We . . . drive fast; we have plenty of time.
5 You . . . drive fast; there is a speed limit here.
6 Candidates . . . bring books into the examination room.
7 You . . . write to him for he will be here tomorrow.
8 We . . . make any noise or we'll wake the baby.
9 You . . . bring an umbrella. It isn't going to rain.
10 You . . . do all the exercise. Ten sentences will be enough.
11 We . . . reheat the pie. We can eat it cold.
12 Mother to child: You . . . tell lies.
13 You . . . turn on the light; I can see quite well.
14 You . . . strike a match; the room is full of gas.
15 You . . . talk to other candidates during the exam.
16 We . . . make any more sandwiches; we have plenty now.
17 You . . . put salt in any of his dishes. Salt is very bad for him.
18 You . . . take anything out of a shop without paying for it.
19 You . . . carry that parcel home yourself; the shop will send it.
20 You . . . clean the windows. The window-cleaner is coming tomorrow.
21 Mother to child: You . . . play with matches.
22 Church notice: Visitors . . . walk about the church during a service.
23 I . . . go to the shops today. There is plenty of food in the house.
24 You . . . smoke in a non-smoking compartment.
25 Police notice: Cars . . . be parked here.
26 We . . . open the lion's cage. It is contrary to Zoo regulations.
27 You . . . make your bed. The maid will do it.
28 I want this letter typed but you . . . do it today. Tomorrow will do.
29 I'll lend you the money and you . . . pay me back till next month.
30 We . . . climb any higher; we can see very well from here.
31 You . . . look under the bed. There isn't anybody there.
32 You . . . ask a woman her age. It's not polite.
33 You've given me too much.
You . . . eat it all.
34 We . . . forget to shut the lift gates.

35 Mother to child: You . . . interrupt when I am speaking.
36 If you want the time, pick up the receiver and dial 123; you . . . say anything.

74 *need not* and *don't have to* etc.

A PEG 143–4

Replace the words underlined by **need not/need I?** etc., or a negative or interrogative **have to** form.

e.g. I've been invited to a wedding; but I can't go. Will it be necessary for me to send a present? *or* Shall I have to send a present?

1 It isn't necessary for him to go on working. He has already reached retiring age. (He . . .)
2 Was it necessary for you to wait a long time for your bus?
3 It isn't necessary for me to water my tomato plants every day.
4 It will be necessary for them to get up early when they go out to work every day.
5 We had to stop at the frontier but we were not required to open our cases.
6 It wasn't necessary to walk. He took us in his car. (We . . .)
7 My employer said, 'I shan't require you tomorrow.' (You . . . come.)
8 It is never necessary for me to work on Saturdays.
9 When I am eighteen I'll be of age. Then it won't be necessary to live at home if I don't want to.
10 Father to son: It isn't necessary for you to call me 'Father'; call me 'Alfred'.
11 Will it be necessary for us to report this accident to the police?
12 When you buy something on the instalment system you are not required to pay the whole price at once.
13 Did you know enough English to ask for your ticket? It wasn't necessary to say anything. I bought my ticket at a machine.
14 It isn't necessary to buy a licence for a bicycle in England. (We . . .)
15 Is it essential for you to finish tonight?
16 Is it necessary for people to go everywhere by boat in Venice?
17 Will it be necessary for me to sleep under a mosquito net?
18 Most people think that civil servants are not required to work very hard.

19 It wasn't necessary to swim. We were able to wade across.
20 When a stranger enters a room the men in the room have to stand up but it isn't necessary for the women to do this.
21 Our plane was delayed so we had lunch at the airport. But it wasn't necessary to pay for the lunch. The airline gave it to us.
22 Is it obligatory for us to vote?
23 When you were a child were you required to practise the piano?
24 I saw the accident but fortunately it wasn't necessary for me to give evidence as there were plenty of other witnesses.
25 Small boy to friend: It won't be necessary for you to work hard when you come to my school. The teachers aren't very strict.
26 They had plenty of time. It wasn't necessary for them to hurry.
27 Is it necessary for you to take your dog with you everywhere?
28 What time was it necessary for you to leave home?
29 I brought my passport but I wasn't required to show it to anyone.
30 I missed one day of the exam. Will it be necessary for me to take the whole exam again.?
31 Is it really necessary for you to practise the violin at 3 a.m.?
32 Everything was done for me. It wasn't necessary for me to do anything.
33 Are French school children obliged to work on Saturdays?
34 I was late for the opera.
Was it necessary for you to wait till the end of the first act before finding your seat?
35 He repaired my old watch so it wasn't necessary for me to buy a new one after all.
36 Were you required to make a speech?

75 *must, can't* and *needn't* with the perfect infinitive

A PEG 134, 146, 151

must + perfect infinitive is used for affirmative deductions.
can't/couldn't + infinitive is used for negative deductions.
needn't + perfect infinitive is used for a past action which was unnecessary but was performed. (See also Exercise 78.)

Fill the spaces in the following sentences by using one of these forms + the perfect infinitive of the verb in brackets.

1 Did you hear me come in last night?
No, I . . . (be) asleep.

2 I wonder who broke the wineglass; it . . . (be) the cat for she was out all day.
3 You . . . (help) him. (you helped him but he didn't need help)
4 I had my umbrella when I came out but I haven't got it now.
You . . . (leave) it on the bus.
5 He . . . (escape) by this window because it is barred.
6 I . . . (give) 10p. 5p would have been enough.
7 I saw a rattlesnake near the river yesterday.
You . . . (see) a rattlesnake. There aren't any rattlesnakes in this country.
8 He is back already.
He . . . (start) very early.
9 He returned home with a tiger cub.
His wife . . . (be) very pleased about that.
10 I bought two bottles of milk.
You . . . (buy) milk; we have heaps in the house.
11 I phoned you at nine this morning but got no answer.
I'm sorry. I . . . (be) in the garden.
12 I left my bicycle here and now it's gone.
Someone . . . (borrow) it.
13 She went to sleep in the park and when she woke up her watch had vanished.
Someone . . . (steal) it while she slept.
14 I've opened another bottle.
You . . . (do) that. We've only just started this one.
15 The machine said, 'You weigh 65 kilos,' and I said, 'Thank you.'
You . . . (say) anything.
16 I told him to turn left and he immediately turned right!
He . . . (understand) you.
17 Perhaps he swam across.
No, he . . . (do) that; he can't swim.
18 Do you remember reading about it in the newspapers?
No, I . . . (be) abroad at the time.
19 He . . . (walk) from here to London in two hours. It isn't possible.
20 He was very sick last night.
The meat we had for supper . . . (be) good.
21 There was a dock strike and the liner couldn't leave port.
The passengers . . . (be) furious.
22 We went to a restaurant and had a very good dinner for 75p.
You . . . (have) a very good dinner if you only paid 75p.
23 I have just watered the roses.
You . . . (water) them. Look, it's raining now!

24 That carpet was made entirely by hand.
It . . . (take) a long time.
25 The door was open.
It . . . (be) open. I had locked it myself and the key was in my pocket.
26 He said that he watered the plants every day.
He . . . (water) them. If he had they wouldn't have died.
27 He came out of the water with little red spots all over his back.
He . . . (be) stung by a jelly-fish.
28 We've sent for a doctor.
You . . . (send) for him. I am perfectly well.
29 I've made two copies.
You . . . (make) two. One would have been enough.
30 There was a terrible crash at 3 a.m.
That . . . (be) Tom coming in from his party.
31 I had to get down the mountain in a thick fog.
That . . . (be) very difficult.
32 I saw Ann in the library yesterday.
You . . . (see) her; she is still abroad.
33 How did he get out of the house? He . . . (come) down the stairs for they were blazing.
34 You . . . (lend) him your map. He has one of his own.
35 I spoke in English, very slowly.
You . . . (speak) slowly. He speaks English very fluently.
36 He was found unconscious at the foot of the cliff. He . . . (fall) 200 metres.

76 *will* and *shall*

A PEG 202, 224–8, 233–4

Put **shall** or **will** in the spaces in the following sentences.

1 Where . . . we go now?
2 . . . you be here when we get back?
3 Next time I go, you . . . come with me. (a promise)
4 . . . you have a cigarette?
5 Where . . . we meet?
6 I . . . have to think it over.
7 'If you want it you . . . have it,' said his father. (a promise)
8 . . . customers please count their change as mistakes cannot be rectified afterwards. (notice in a shop)

9 Who will go to the shops for me?
I . . . .
10 . . . we have a picnic on the beach?
11 We . . . know the result in a week's time.
12 If you press that button the engine . . . start.
13 I've got a hole in my shoe. I . . . have to have it repaired.
14 School notice: All new boys . . . report to the headmaster.
15 We'll leave the light on so that he . . . not have any difficulty in finding his room.
16 'If there is any cake left you . . . have it,' promised his aunt.
17 Notice above a box-office: . . . patrons please examine their tickets as tickets cannot be exchanged afterwards.
18 I am determined that my boy . . . have a better start than I had.
19 Some people . . . try to cross a busy road against the traffic lights.
20 Police notice: . . . anyone who saw this accident please telephone the nearest police station?
21 Clause in a lease: The tenant . . . be responsible for all repairs.
22 . . . I write my address on the back?
23 They have put lights on the barricade so that motorists . . . not bump into it.
24 It's very dark in here.
So it is; I . . . turn on the light.
25 What . . . I say?
26 You forgot to post your letter.
So I did. I . . . go back and post it now.
27 Clause in a lease: Tenants . . . not play any musical instrument after midnight.
28 I . . . not be able to carry it by myself.
I . . . help you.
29 Committee regulations: Ten members . . . constitute a quorum at any meeting.
30 She said, 'I . . . not fill up this form. The questions are impertinent.'
31 He said, 'If you don't do it you . . . be fined.'
32 If you . . . kindly wait a moment I'll see what can be done.
33 You . . . not be late, . . . you?
34 You've helped me tremendously and you . . . not regret it. (*i.e. I'll reward you*)
35 I . . . be leaving Victoria tomorrow at 8.00 a.m.
I . . . come and see you off.
36 Who . . . I say called?
You needn't mention any name. He . . . know who I am.

77 *would* and *should*

A PEG 235–8, 224–7, 309–10

Put **should** or **would** in the spaces in the following sentences.

1 . . . you mind opening the door?
2 . . . you like another cup of coffee?
3 He insisted that the newspaper . . . print an apology.
4 The old admiral . . . sit for hours watching the ships.
5 . . . you be so good as to keep an eye on my house while I am away?
6 I . . . say nothing about it if I were you.
7 That hat doesn't suit you; you . . . buy another.
8 If you pulled the communication cord the train . . . stop and you . . . be fined £25.
9 They went to the cinema at 2.30, so they . . . be back here by 6.00.
10 . . . you please help me with this?
11 It is very strange that he . . . think that.
12 I wish he . . . not play his radio so loudly.
13 . . . you be very kind and lend me your typewriter?
14 I . . . like to know where you have been.
15 It was decided that the matter . . . be referred to a special committee.
16 Perhaps you . . . be kind enough to let us know about this.
17 If the telephone . . . ring please say that I'll be back at six.
18 . . . you like to come or . . . you rather stay here?
19 There are too many accidents. Everyone . . . be much more careful.
20 Their method was always the same; they . . . wait till their victim had left the bank and then go up to him and ask for a light.
21 What are you doing here? You . . . be in bed.
22 It is essential that this matter . . . be kept out of the newspapers.
23 He suggested that the money . . . be raised by public subscription.
24 If you . . . change your mind, this address will always find me.
25 If this machine . . . at any time fail to give complete satisfaction please post us the enclosed card.
26 He changed his name so that nobody . . . know what he had been before.
27 If he offered me money I . . . refuse.
28 I wish you . . . not ask so many questions.
29 He ordered that Tom . . . leave the house at once.
30 Shall I help you?
If you . . . I . . . be most grateful.

31 He is anxious that everyone . . . understand why he acted as he did.
32 You . . . not argue with your father; you . . . obey him.
33 He was a very patient cat; he . . . sit for hours beside a mousehole.
34 . . . the pain return take one of these pills.
35 It is most important that I . . . see him at once.
36 They didn't dare leave the train in case they . . . be left behind.

78 *would* and *should*

A PEG 235–8, 224–7, 309–10

Put **should** or **would** in the spaces in the following sentences:

1 It is only fair that you . . . know the truth about your own father and it is better that you . . . hear it from me than from some stranger.
2 If you . . . kindly wait here a moment I'll ring the director's office.
3 . . . these measures fail to restore order harsher restrictions will have to be imposed.
4 The rocks were icy and he was terrified lest he . . . slip.
5 If Pierre liked any dish he . . . send for the chef and congratulate him, and if anything was wrong he . . . send for the manager and complain.
An Englishman . . . never dare to do that; he . . . be too shy.
6 I was just burying the bones in the garden when who . . . look over the hedge but the village policeman.
7 When he found out that the man had smallpox he urged that every effort . . . be made to contact his fellow passengers.
8 I wish you . . . go out or sit down. How . . . you like it if I kept tramping round when you were trying to work?
9 I've just received an anonymous threatening letter. What . . . I do about it?
I . . . take it to the police if I were you.
10 The committee thinks that you have been guilty of disloyalty.
I don't know why the committee . . . think that.
11 I can't repair it now but if you . . . like to leave it with me I'll see what can be done.
12 You complained to the manager, of course?
No, I asked to speak to him but he . . . not come to the phone.
You . . . have insisted.
13 Where will he be now?
Oh, he . . . be there by now; the flight only takes an hour.

14 If your main parachute . . . fail to open your second one will open automatically.
15 I suggested that Tom . . . walk on and try to get help while I stayed with the injured man but he . . . not hear of this.
16 I am amazed that you . . . even suggest offering bribes.
17 This passage doesn't lead anywhere. It is odd that no one . . . have noticed this before.
18 . . . you mind not smoking; this is the petrol store.
Then there . . . be a 'No Smoking' notice.
19 Can't I trust you not to read my letters? It is ridiculous that I . . . have to lock things up in my own house.
20 He said he wished I . . . not come so often.
21 This train is entirely automatic; there is no driver; but a mechanic is always available in case anything . . . go wrong.
22 She had one rather boring habit; she . . . insist on telling people about her dreams.
23 He recommended that the trouble makers in the factory . . . be dismissed.
24 It is absurd that women . . . be paid less than men for doing the same work.
25 I . . . rather you asked him. Last time I tried to speak to him he . . . not listen.
26 When he went out he left the radio on so that his parents . . . think that he was still in his room.
27 He was determined that his children . . . go to the best schools available.
28 Tom says you are foolish to take such a risk.
He . . .! (*That is typical of him.*)
29 When four hours had passed and there was still no sign of him she began to be worried lest he . . . have met with some accident.
30 People are very fond of saying, 'This . . . be stopped', or, 'Something . . . be done about this', but if they were the government they . . . not know how to stop it or what to do about it.
31 It is amazing that the Leaning Tower of Pisa . . . have stood for so long.
32 He resigned from the government in order that everyone . . . know that he disapproved of the new policy.
33 If I had had his education and he had had mine perhaps I . . . be sitting at his desk and he . . . be out here sweeping the streets.
34 He was a terribly obstinate child, who . . . never obey the simplest order, but . . . argue every point till she nearly went mad.
35 Robinson said, 'Why . . . Smith get all the credit when someone else

has done all the work?'

36 All day he . . . sit in his office immaculately dressed, but at night he . . . put on dirty ragged clothing and roam about the streets with disreputable companions.

79 Auxiliary verbs used with the perfect infinitive

A PEG 146–7, 151–2, 255

Use the perfect infinitive of the verb in italics with the appropriate auxiliary. Phrases underlined should not be repeated but their meaning should be expressed by auxiliary + perfect infinitive.

e.g. You (*bought*) bread, which was not necessary.
You needn't have bought bread.

1 To someone who was not at the party: 'We had a wonderful time; you (*be*) there.'

2 He thinks that it is possible that Shakespeare (*write*) it.
Shakespeare (*not write*) it because events are mentioned that didn't occur till after Shakespeare's time.

3 I found this baby bird at the foot of a tree.
It (*fall*) from a nest.

4 I used to visit her and I always wondered why she had those dreadful pictures on the walls.
It is possible that she (*like*) them.

5 During the gale, the captain was on the bridge the whole time.
He (*be*) exhausted afterwards.

6 You (*send*) a telegram, which was quite unnecessary; a letter would have done.

7 You (*leave*) a note. (It was very inconsiderate of you not to do so.)

8 Somebody phoned at lunchtime but I couldn't catch the name.
It (*be*) my brother. He sometimes rings me up then.

9 The lecturer was a tall thin man with white hair.
Then it (*not be*) Dr Fell because he is short and fat. It (*be*) Dr Jones; I think he is thin.

10 You (*not go*) out yesterday without a coat. No wonder you caught cold.

11 I saw them in the street but they didn't stop to speak to me.
It is possible that they (*be*) in a hurry.

12 They (*be*) married next week but now they have quarrelled and the wedding has been cancelled.

13 If we hadn't had this puncture we (*be*) home by now.
14 You (*carry*) the dog, which was unnecessary. He can walk very well.
15 People were waiting but the bus didn't stop.
It is possible that it (*be*) full.
16 We went sailing on a lake in a London park. I think it was the Round Pond.
It (*not be*) the Round Pond. There are only toy boats there. It (*be*) the Serpentine.
17 Look, there's a tree right across the road!
So there is. It (*be*) blown down by the gale last night.
18 This building (*be*) finished by the end of last year, (this was the plan) but there have been so many strikes that it isn't finished yet.
19 If the tempest hadn't struck them they (*reach*) the top next day.
20 You (*cross*) the road by the subway. (but you didn't)
21 It is a pity you (*not bring*) your kite. It is just the day for kites.
22 It is possible that I (*be*) mistaken.
23 I sat on a seat in the park and now my coat is covered in green stripes.
The paint (*be*) wet.
24 I suppose it was Charles who left the kitchen in such a mess.
No, it (*not be*) Charles. He never has a meal in. It (*be*) Bill.
25 I know she was in because I heard her radio, but she didn't open the door.
Possibly she (*not hear*) the bell.
26 If you had told me that you were in London I (*put*) you up. (this would have been possible)
27 If they had gone any further they (*fall*) over a precipice.
28 He (*check*) that his brakes were working properly. (but he didn't)
29 You (*apologize*), which was not necessary.
30 I can't think why they didn't try to help him.
It is possible that they (*not realize*) that he was drowning.
31 He (*thank*) us. (we are offended that he didn't)
32 I (*go*) on Tuesday (this was the plan). But on Tuesday I had a terrible cold so I decided to wait till Wednesday.
33 You (*warn*) him that the ice was dangerous. (but you didn't)
34 If you had kept quiet nobody (*know*) anything about it.
35 You *bought* a new one, which wasn't necessary. I could have lent you mine.
36 As soon as I switched on my new electric cooker there was an explosion.
There (*be*) something wrong with it.

5 Indirect speech and passive voice

80 Indirect speech: statements

C PEG 293–6

1 Students are asked to assume that these sentences are spoken and reported on different days. This will mean that a sentence such as: He said, 'I am coming *tomorrow*,' will become: He said that he was coming *the next day*, and so on.
This applies to all the exercises on indirect speech in this book.

2 With indirect speech, when the person addressed is mentioned, **tell** is more usual than **say to** as an introductory verb.

e.g. *He told me that he was going away the next day*, is more usual than *He said to me that he was going away the next day*.

Put the following into indirect speech.

1 'I have something to show you,' I said to her.
2 'Nothing grows in my garden. It never gets any sun,' she said.
3 'I'm going away tomorrow, mother,' he said.
4 'I've been in London for a month but so far I haven't had time to visit the Tower,' said Rupert.
5 'It isn't so foggy today as it was yesterday,' I remarked.
6 'The new underpass is being officially opened the day after tomorrow,' said the BBC announcer.
7 'We have moved into our new flat. We don't like it nearly so much as our last one,' said my aunt.
8 'We have a lift but very often it doesn't work,' they said.
9 'From one of the windows of my flat I can see the Eiffel Tower,' said my friend.
10 'I've no idea what the time is but I'll dial 123 and find out,' said his daughter.
11 He said, 'My wife has just been made a judge.'
12 'I'll come with you as soon as I am ready,' she replied.
13 'I have a German lesson this afternoon and I haven't done my homework yet,' said the small boy.

14 'If you let the iron get too hot you will scorch your clothes,' I warned her.
15 'You haven't given me quite enough. The bill is for £14 and you've paid me only £13,' he pointed out.
16 Ann said, 'Englishmen make good husbands because they are nearly always willing to help in the house.'
17 Mary answered, 'I like men to be useful but I don't like them to be too domesticated. I prefer them to keep out of the kitchen altogether. Men look silly in aprons anyway.'
18 Motoring report: The new Rolls Royce runs so quietly that all you can hear is the ticking of the clock.
Managing director of the Rolls Royce company: In that case we'll have to do something about the clock.
19 'I don't know what to do with all my plums. I suppose I'll have to make jam. The trouble is that no one in my family eats jam,' she said.
20 'We like working on Sundays because we get double pay,' explained the builders.
21 He said, 'I am quite a good cook and I do all my own washing and mending too.'
22 'You can keep that one if you like, Joan,' she said. 'I've got plenty of others.'
23 'I'm going fishing with mother this afternoon,' said the small boy, 'and we are going into the garden now to dig for worms.'
24 'You've got my umbrella,' I said crossly. 'Yours is in your bedroom.'
25 'I know exactly what they said,' the private detective explained to his client, 'because I put a tape-recorder under the table.'
26 'I'll sit up till she comes in, but I hope she won't be late,' said Mrs Pitt.
27 'If you give me some wire, I'll hang that picture for you,' said my cousin.
28 'I have a Turkish bath occasionally, but it doesn't seem to make any difference to my weight,' she said.

81 Indirect speech: statements

B PEG 293–6

Tenses which do not change when direct speech becomes indirect:

1 If the introductory verb is in the present, present perfect or future tense all verb tenses remain unchanged (see PEG 276).

2 Even when the introductory verb is in the past tense, certain tenses sometimes remain unchanged:

a The past continuous tense normally remains unchanged except when it is the only verb in the sentence or when it refers to a completed action (see no. 13).

b The past tense remains unchanged in the following cases:

i In time clauses.

When a sentence contains a time clause whose verb is in the past (or past continuous) tense, both the verb in the time clause and the main verb of the sentence normally remain unchanged:

e.g. *He said, 'I dropped it while I was running'* becomes: *He said that he dropped it while he was running*, though it is possible sometimes, especially when the time clause verb is in the past continuous, to put the main verb into the past perfect tense:

e.g. *He said that he had dropped it while he was running*.

ii A past tense used to describe a state of affairs which still exists when the speech is reported, normally remains unchanged (see example no. 24 below).

iii **would**, **should**, **used**, **might**, and **could** (except when it means **was able**) normally remain unchanged in statements (for **must** see Exercise 88).

iv Past subjunctives remains unchanged. Therefore:

conditional sentences type 2 remain unchanged
would rather + past tense remains unchanged
you had better + infinitive remains unchanged, or is reported by **advise** + object + verb
past tenses after **wish** and **it is time** remain unchanged.

Put the following into indirect speech, being careful to avoid ambiguity:

1 'I couldn't get into the house because I had lost my key, so I had to break a window,' he said.
2 'The mirror is there so that you can see yourself when you are dancing,' explained the instructress to the pupil.
3 'I wrote to him the day before yesterday. I wonder why he hasn't rung up,' she said.

4 'This is quite a good model, madam. I use one of them myself,' said the shop assistant.
5 'If I had spoken to my father as you speak to me he'd have beaten me,' he said to me.
6 'If you want seats you'd better apply early. I once tried a week before the performance and the theatre was all booked up,' she said to him.
7 'We walked 50 miles last night to see the Minister and protest about our rents being raised. He was very polite and promised to do what he could for us,' said one of the tenants.
8 'One day I'll drop dead and then you'll be sorry,' she said.
9 'My new house is supposed to be haunted but so far I haven't seen any ghosts,' said the woman.
10 In Shakespeare's *Othello* Iago says, 'I will wear my heart upon my sleeve.'
11 'If it rains this afternoon it will be too wet to play the match tomorrow,' the captain said.
12 'I meant to plug in the electric blanket but I plugged in the electric kettle by mistake. I'm always doing silly things like that,' she told her guest.
13 'I was intending to do it tomorrow,' he said, 'but now I don't think I'll be able to.'
14 'I'm sure your son will do very well at the university, Mrs Smith,' said the headmaster. 'He's done very well here.'
15 'Nothing I can do pleases your father. I don't think he likes me,' said the young wife.
'You mustn't think that,' said her husband; 'it is just that he is old and finds it hard to get used to new people.' (leave **mustn't** unchanged)
16 'The steak is overdone again. I'm not complaining; I'm just pointing it out,' said her husband.
17 'They couldn't open the safe on the spot so they carried it away with them,' the night watchman reported.
18 'If you saw my father, you'd recognize him at once. He is the most extraordinary-looking man,' she said to me.
19 'I found an old Roman coin in the garden yesterday,' he said, 'and I'm going to take it to the museum this afternoon.'
20 He said, 'I got out of my boat, leaving the engine running, but while I was standing on the quay the gears suddenly engaged themselves and the boat went straight out of the harbour with no one on board.'
21 Then Macbeth enters and says, 'I have done the deed.'
22 The advertisement said, 'If you arrange these slogans in the correct

order you may win twenty pounds a week for life.'

23 My brother said, 'You may take my car if you like. I shan't be needing it tomorrow or the day after.'

24 'Yesterday Tom and I went to look at a house that he was thinking of buying. It was rather a nice house and had a lovely garden but Tom decided against it because it was opposite a cemetery,' said Celia.

25 He said, 'My wife wants to take a job but I'd rather she concentrated on our home.'

26 'I don't know what your father will say when he sees what a mess your puppies have made of this five-pound note,' said my mother.

27 'It's high time you passed your test; I am tired of driving round with an L-plate on the front of the car,' my sister said.

28 He said, 'If I press my ear against the wall I can hear what the people in the next flat are saying.'

82 Indirect speech: questions

C PEG 300

Put the following into indirect speech.

1 'Why are you looking through the keyhole?' I said.

2 'Who put salt in my coffee?' he asked.

3 'Which of you knows how to make Irish stew?' said the chief cook.

4 'Why did you travel first class?' I asked him.

5 'How can I possibly run in these high-heeled shoes?' she enquired.

6 'What is your new house like?' I asked them.

7 He said, 'Where am I supposed to go now?'

8 'Whose car did you borrow last night?' I said to him.

9 'What was she wearing when you saw her last?' the policeman asked me.

10 'Who owns this revolver?' said the detective.

11 'Where were you last night, Mr Jones?' he said.

12 'What else did you see?' I asked the boy.

13 'Have you done this sort of work before?' said his new employer.

14 'Can you read the last line on the chart?' the oculist asked her.

15 'Did they understand what you said to them?' he inquired.

16 'Are you being attended to, sir?' said the shop assistant.

17 'Will you go on strike when the others do?' the shop steward asked him.

18 'Do you see what I see, Mary?' said the young man.

19 'Who left the banana skin on the front doorstep?' said my mother.

20 'Have you gone completely mad?' I asked. 'Do you want to blow us all up?'
21 'Why is his house so full of large leather couches?' she asked. 'Was his father a psychiatrist?'
22 'Are you leaving today or tomorrow morning?' said his secretary.
23 'How far is it?' I said, 'and how long will it take me to get there?'
24 'Could I speak to Mrs Pitt?' said the caller.
'I'm afraid she's out,' said the *au pair* girl. 'Could I take a message?'
25 'Are you sorry for what you did?' the mother asked the little boy.
26 'Are you going to see him off at the station?' I asked her.
27 'Would you mind if I looked inside your bag, Madam?' said the policeman.
28 'If someone fell at your feet foaming at the mouth would you know what to do?' said the instructor in First Aid.

83 Indirect speech: questions

B PEG 299–300

1 Be careful of questions beginning **shall I** (see PEG 279).

2 'Yes' and 'No' answers are usually expressed in indirect speech by the subject + the appropriate auxiliary verb.

e.g. He said, 'Do you like it?' She said, 'Yes.'
He asked her if she liked it and she said that she did.

Put the following into indirect speech:

1 'Are you going to let me in or aren't you?' said the young man.
2 'Did you go to France for your holidays after all or did you stay at home?' he asked her.
3 'What shall I do with your mail when you are away?' asked his landlady. 'Shall I forward it?'
4 'What would you wish for if a wizard suddenly appeared and offered you three wishes?' said the small boy.
5 'Shall I ever understand women?' he asked himself.
6 'Will you be here for the next ten minutes?' she said.
'Yes,' I answered.
7 'Could I lose five kilos in one week?' the fat woman asked.
'No,' said the doctor.
8 'Shall I ask her to wait?' said his secretary.

9 'Aren't you tired of living in an ice-box?' said the television advertiser. 'Why don't you install our central heating?'

10 'Haven't you got a television set?' he asked.
'No', I said. 'Nobody in our village has got one.'
'How can you bear to live in such a backward place?' he said.

11 'Wouldn't you like to look ten years younger?' said my hairdresser.
'No,' I replied.

12 'Shall I tell him what happened?' she said, 'or shall I say nothing?'
'Why do you ask me?' I said. 'Why don't you ask your solicitor?'

13 'Have you good hearing and sight?' the form asked, 'and do you suffer from dizziness or black-outs?'

14 'Do you know anybody in this area or could you get a reference from your previous landlady?' he asked me.

15 'Have you ever been convicted of driving while under the influence of drink?' she asked him.
'No,' he said.

16 'Do you have many suicides in your country? Do you think suicide is a crime?' the students were asked.

17 'Do you think the fog's going to get thicker and what shall we do if it does?' said Tom.
'If it gets worse we'll have to leave the car and walk home,' said his uncle.

18 'Would you like to see over the house or are you more interested in the garden?' she asked me.

19 'Would you like to wait or would you rather come back tomorrow?' said the official.

20 'Shall I be in time?' he asked himself, looking at his watch.

21 'I've just received my son's school report. Would you like to see it?' he asked.
'No,' I said.

22 'Will you be able to guide me or shall I bring a map?' he said.

23 'Shall we ever see each other again?' he said.

24 'When you don't like a film do you stay to the end or walk out in the middle?' she asked.

25 'What makes you think Smith is going to resign? Has he told you so or are you only guessing? Would you like to take over his job?' asked my colleague.

26 'Do you find it stuffy in here, sir? Shall I open the window?' said the waiter.

27 'Did you hear a terrible crash about 3 a.m. this morning?' said my host.
'Yes,' I said. 'What was it?'

28 'If you had to be an animal,' I asked her, 'what animal would you choose to be?'

84 Indirect speech: commands
C PEG 301

Put the following into indirect speech.

1 He said, 'Get out of my way.'
2 'Climb in through the window,' he ordered.
3 'Please pay at the desk,' said the assistant.
4 'Open your bag, please,' said the store detective.
5 'Don't worry about anything, Mrs Pitt,' said her solicitor. 'Leave it all to me.'
6 'Don't use bent coins in a slot machine,' I advised him.
7 'Follow that car,' the detective said to the taxi-driver.
8 'Wash it in lukewarm water,' recommended the assistant.
9 'Have confidence in me,' urged the doctor.
10 'Take me up to the 33rd floor,' he said to the liftman.
11 'Read the notice about life-saving equipment,' advised the air-hostess.
12 'Always cook with butter,' said her mother, 'never use margarine.'
13 'Don't argue with your father,' I said.
14 'Don't make a sound,' he said in a whisper.
15 'Wait for me at the bridge,' said the young man.
16 'Don't eat too much starch,' I advised her, 'and avoid fried food.'
17 'Don't say anything to make her angry,' said my father.
18 Notice: Please do not ask at the desk for change for telephone calls.
19 'Don't forget to feed the goldfish,' Mary said to her brother.
20 'Get your dog a bigger basket,' he said.
21 'Write to me as often as you can,' said his wife.
22 'Put your pistol on the table,' said the crook.
23 'Please book me a seat in a non-smoker,' said the traveller.
24 'Don't forget your sandwiches,' said his mother.
25 'Don't go near the water, children,' she said.
26 'Search the house,' said the police sergeant.
27 'Don't make mountains out of molehills,' he said.
28 'Put down that gun. It's loaded,' he said.

85 Indirect speech: commands

C PEG 301

Put the following into indirect speech.

1 'Make good use of your time. You won't get such an opportunity again,' he said to us.
2 'Don't wait till tomorrow,' said the advertisement, 'post the coupon today.'
3 'Be very careful crossing roads,' she said, 'and remember that they drive on the left in England.'
4 'I can't open it. You have a try, Peter,' he said.
5 'Go and get me a paper, and come straight back,' he said to me.
6 'Someone's coming. Get into the cupboard,' she said.
7 'Give way to traffic approaching from your right,' the road sign warned us.
8 'Please send whatever you can spare. All contributions will be acknowledged immediately,' said the secretary of the disaster fund.
9 'Wear a wig and no one will know who you are,' I advised him.
10 'Don't bathe when the red flag is flying,' said the lifeguard.
11 'Don't forget to thank Mrs Jones when you are saying goodbye to her,' said his mother.
12 'Watch the milk and don't let it boil over,' he said.
13 'Don't shelter under a tree in a thunderstorm,' he said. 'The tree might be struck by lightning.
14 'Put the message into a bottle and throw it into the sea,' said my companion on the raft.
15 'Read it for yourself if you don't believe what I say,' he told me.
16 'Stop that dog, he's got my slipper!' shouted my mother.
17 'Don't drive too fast or the baby'll be sick,' she said to her husband.
18 'Do make the coffee a bit stronger,' I begged. 'It was terribly weak last night.'
19 'Do something, don't just stand about,' she said to me.
20 'Smell this. Do you think it has gone bad?' she said.
21 'Don't take your coat off. We are going out again in a moment,' she told him.
22 'Stand by the window and tell me if anyone goes into the house opposite,' he said.
23 'Don't move till the policeman waves you on,' said the driving instructor.
24 'Don't touch it. You will make it worse,' he told me.

25 'Be careful; the steps are very slippery,' I warned him.
26 'Ask him to ring me back,' said the caller.
'Wait a moment,' said the girl, rummaging for a pencil. 'Now could you repeat that, please?'
27 'Tell them not to work too fast,' said the workman. 'If we finish before six we shan't get any overtime.'
28 'Prepare to meet your doom. The end of the world is at hand,' said the placard.

86 Indirect speech: commands with *if*- clauses and time clauses

B PEG 302

Commands with **if-** clauses or time clauses,

e.g. 'If it gets cold give him another blanket.'
'When it gets dark light the lantern and hang it out,'

can be expressed in indirect speech:

1 by **tell** + infinitive + **if**/time clause (usually in that order).

e.g. He told me to give her another blanket if it got cold.
I told him to light the lantern, etc., when it got dark.

Sometimes however (as in nos. 5 and 10 below) the **tell** construction would produce rather a clumsy sentence. It is then advisable to use the **say** construction below.

2 by **say** + { **was to** / **should** } + **if**/time clause

e.g. He said that if it got cold I was to/should give her, etc.
I said that when it got dark he was to/should light, etc.

was to expresses a definite command; **should** implies advice.

Put the following into indirect speech:

1 He said, 'When you are at the butcher's remember to get a bone for the dog.'
2 She said, 'If you feel faint sit down and put your head between your knees.'
3 'If I find your purse what shall I do with it?' he said.
'Keep it till you see me again,' I replied.

4 She said, 'If he arrives before I get back give him something to drink.'
5 'If anyone rings up,' she said, 'say that I'll be back shortly.'
6 'When you are driving always look in your driving mirror before turning right,' said my instructor.
7 'Leave the key under the mat if you go out,' she said.
8 'If you think the room is cold shut the windows,' said my aunt.
9 'If you feel lonely any time ring me up,' he said.
10 'If she doesn't want cabbage ask her if she'd like some cauliflower,' he said to me.
11 'Get the car off the road on to the verge if you have a puncture. Don't leave it on the road,' said my father.
12 'If I am not back by this time tomorrow take this letter to the police,' he said.
13 'When you see Mrs Pitt don't forget to thank her,' she said to her husband.
14 'When the bell rings take the meat out of the oven,' my sister said.
15 'If you are taken prisoner,' said the officer, 'give your name, rank and number but refuse to answer any other questions.'
16 'When you hear the fire alarm, shut all windows and go downstairs as quickly as possible,' said the schoolmaster.
17 'If the lift should stop between two floors press the emergency button,' he said.
18 'Before you allow anyone to use the Turkish bath remember to ask him if he has a weak heart,' said the senior attendant.

87 Indirect speech: sentences with suggestions and commands with *let*

A PEG 303

1 First person imperative
He said, 'Let's go' usually becomes:
a *He suggested going*
though possible in certain cases are:
b *He suggested that they should go*
c *He urged/advised them to go.*
He said, 'Let's not go' can be expressed by any of these constructions in the negative; but **suggest** + negative gerund is slightly less usual than the others and is often replaced by the (b) type of construction or by:
He was against going/against the idea/against it.
He was opposed to the idea/He opposed the idea, etc.

2 Third person imperative
He said, 'Let them go,' can become:
a *He suggested that they should go/suggested their going*
but usually it expresses an obligation and becomes:
b *He said that they should go/ought to go.*
Very occasionally it expresses a command and becomes:
c *He said that they were to go.*

3 Second person suggestions
These are usually made with **suggest** or with such phrases as: 'suppose you go,' 'why don't you go?' 'what about you going?', etc. In indirect speech these become: *He suggested that I should go/suggested my going/advised me to go.*

let is also an ordinary verb meaning **allow**.
e.g. *'Let me go!' the boy said to the policeman.*
The boy asked the policeman to let him go.

Put the following into indirect speech:

1 'Let's go to the cinema,' said Ann.
2 The Prime Minister said, 'Let us show the nation that we are worthy of their confidence.' (**urged**)
3 'Let me stay up a little longer tonight, mother,' begged the child.
4 'I've worked for you for ten years,' said the man. 'What about giving me a rise?'
5 The police officer said, 'Let's leave the wrecked car here for a bit. It may remind other drivers to be more careful.'
6 'I've helped you every time up to now,' said his teacher. 'Why don't you try to do the next one by yourself?'
7 'Let no one speak to that man,' said the strike leader. 'He is a blackleg.'
8 'Tom made this mess. Let him clear it up,' said his father.
9 'Get yourself some new clothes,' I suggested.
10 'I can't go with you today,' said the guide, 'but suppose you go by yourselves? It's quite a safe route.'
11 'Let's give a party,' said Ann.
'Let's not,' said her husband.
12 I said, 'Let's not jump to conclusions. Let's wait till we hear confirmation of this rumour.'
13 'Suppose you stop working now and go to bed?' he said. 'You'll be much fresher in the morning.'
14 'Let the nations forget their differences and work together for peace,' said the preacher.

15 'Let me explain,' she said. 'Don't be in such a hurry.'
16 'Let the children play in the garden if they want to,' she told the gardener. 'I'm sure they won't do any harm.'
17 'Let's stay here till the storm has passed,' I said.
18 'It's the government's fault. Let them do something about it,' grumbled my father.

88 Indirect speech: sentences with *must, needn't* and *have to*

A PEG 306

must, *1st person*
'I must' can remain unchanged but usually becomes **had to** though **would have to** is better for an obligation which has only just arisen or is likely to arise in the future.

e.g. Reading the letter he said, 'Good heavens! I *must* go at once!'
He said, 'If she gets worse I *must* stay with her.'

These would become respectively:

He said that he'd *have to* go, and:
He said that he'd *have to* stay.

'Must I?' usually becomes **had to**.
'I must not' usually remains unchanged.

must, *2nd and 3rd person*
'You/he must' usually remains unchanged.
'Must you/he?' usually becomes **had to**.
'You/he must not' remains unchanged or becomes **weren't to/wasn't to**.
must used for permanent commands or prohibitions or to express advice always remains unchanged.
must used to express deduction never changes.

needn't
'I needn't' can change to **didn't have to/wouldn't have to** in the same way that **'I must'** changes to **'had to/would have to**, but it very often remains unchanged.

'You/he needn't' usually remains unchanged.
'Need I/you/he?' remains unchanged or becomes **had to**.

have to

Forms with **have to** follow the usual rules. Remember that **'had to'** in direct speech will become **had had to** in indirect.

e.g. He said, 'After the lecture I *had to* rush home.'
He said that after the lecture he *had had to* rush home.

Put the following into indirect speech.

1 He said, 'If what you say is true I must go to the police.'
2 He said, 'I must be at the docks at six a.m. tomorrow.'
3 'Must you make such a noise?' he asked.
4 'You mustn't come in without knocking,' he told us.
5 'Your ticket will cost £5,' I said.
'In that case,' said my nephew, 'I must go to the bank tomorrow.'
6 Park notice: Dogs must be kept on a lead.
7 His father said, 'He must work harder next term.'
8 'You needn't come in tomorrow,' said my employer. 'Take the day off.'
9 'I must go to the dentist tomorrow,' he said. 'I have an appointment.'
10 Notice: Passengers must not lean out of the window.
11 He said, 'There must be someone in the house; there's smoke coming from the chimney.'
12 She said, 'When you are a big boy you'll have to tie your own shoes.'
13 'Port wine must never be shaken,' my wine-merchant said.
14 'He hasn't had anything to eat since breakfast; he must be starving,' she said.
15 The official said, 'This passport photo isn't like you at all. You must have another one taken.'
16 'You mustn't play with knives, children,' said their mother.
17 'I needn't get up till nine tomorrow,' I said.
18 Railway regulations: Passengers must be in possession of a valid ticket before travelling.
19 'How did you get your bulldog up the escalator?' I said.
'I carried him,' said Tom.
'You must be very strong,' I said admiringly.
20 'You mustn't tell anyone what I've just told you,' she said to me.
21 'Need I eat it all, mummy?' said the child.
'Yes, dear, you must,' she said.
22 'I had to drive your pigs out of my garden,' she said.
23 'Sticks and umbrellas must be left at the desk,' said the notice in the museum.

24 'Must you do it all tonight? Couldn't you leave some for tomorrow?' I asked her.
25 'When you go through Bayeux you must see the tapestry,' he told me.
26 He said, 'You must walk faster, you are far too slow.'
27 'You mustn't forget to put the stamp on or your friend will have to pay double postage,' he told me.
28 'I needn't tell you how grateful I am,' he said.

89 Indirect speech: sentences with *will* and *shall*, *would* and *should*

B PEG 299–302

Put the following into indirect speech.

1 He said, 'Will you come to tea on Monday?'
'Thanks very much,' I said. 'I'd love to.' (I thanked him and . . .)
2 'Will you have another cup of coffee?' said Ann.
'No, thanks,' I said.
3 Notice: In the event of an emergency an alarm bell will be rung and all passengers will assemble at their respective assembly points.
4 'It's seven,' he said. 'She'll be at home now. What about ringing her up?'
5 'Take these letters to the post, will you,' he said, 'and shut the door as you go out.'
6 'Will you help me or shall I ask someone else?' he said.
7 'Will you help me, please?' she said. 'I can't lift it by myself.'
8 'If he asks me where you are what shall I say?' said the secretary.
'Tell him I've gone away on business,' said her employer.
9 'Where shall we all be in ten years' time?' he said.
10 'The milkman is at the door. Shall I pay him?' she said.
11 'I've broken the teapot Ann gave me for Christmas. What shall I do?' she asked.
'I should try to get it mended,' I said. (I advised . . .)
12 'Would you mind moving your car?' he said.
13 'What shall I do if he refuses to let me in?' he said.
'Write a note and push it under the door,' I replied.
14 'Will you be quiet for a moment,' said his exasperated mother.
15 'Would you mind cooking your own supper tonight?' said my landlady.

16 'Look at this dreadful letter. How shall I answer it?' she said.
'I shouldn't answer it at all,' I said.
17 Police announcement: Will anyone who saw this accident please ring 741-6300.
18 'If you will kindly sit down the fortune-teller will be with you in a moment,' the girl said.

90 Indirect speech: mixed types

A PEG 304–5

Exclamations, etc.
Some exclamations can be changed into indirect speech by merely adding a verb;

e.g. He said, 'What a pity!' He said that it was a pity.
He said, 'How marvellous!' He said that it was marvellous.

Others can best be expressed by:

e.g. He exclaimed with delight/horror/surprise, etc.
He gave an exclamation of delight/horror, etc.

Note:

He said, 'Thank you.'	He thanked me.
He said, 'Curse the fog!'	He cursed the fog.
He said, 'Good morning!'	He greeted me/wished me a good morning.
He said, 'Happy Christmas.'	He wished me a happy Christmas.
He said, 'Congratulations!'	He congratulated me.
He said, 'Liar.'	He called me a liar.

Put the following into indirect speech, avoiding as far as possible the verb **say** and using instead such verbs as: **hope, explain, protest, beg, ask, congratulate, interrupt, warn, greet, give, introduce, remark, invite, threaten, point out, insist, offer, refuse, accept, curse, advise, assure, answer, agree, admit,** etc.

1 He said, 'Don't walk on the ice, it isn't safe.'
2 'Miss Brown, this is Miss White. Miss White, Miss Brown,' he said.
3 'Here's twenty pence. Go and get yourself an ice-cream,' I said.

4 'Please, please, do as I say,' I said.
5 'If I were you I'd pretend to be ill for a fortnight,' I said.
6 Tom: I'll pay.
Ann: Oh no, you mustn't.
Tom: I insist on paying.
7 'Come in and look round. There is no obligation to buy,' said the shopkeeper.
8 'Have a cigarette,' he said.
'No, thanks,' I replied.
9 'Curse this map! It's led me wrong again,' he said.
10 'Could you come to dinner tomorrow night?' he asked.
'Thanks very much; I'd love to.'
11 'Could you show me how to work it? I'm not used to electric typewriters,' she said.
12 'You pressed the wrong button,' said the mechanic, 'Don't do it again. You might have a nasty accident.'
13 'What a nuisance! Now I'll have to do it all over again,' he exclaimed.
14 'Suppose you children go out for a nice long walk,' she said.
15 'Hurray, I've passed my exam!' he cried.
'Congratulations!' I said.
16 'Always be polite to people you pass on the way up,' the old politician advised the young diplomat, 'in case you meet them again on your way down.'
17 'Many happy returns of your birthday,' we said.
'Thank you,' said the boy.
18 'You never listen to your mother,' she said in a complaining tone, 'and it's a bit hard after all the trouble I've had bringing you up.'
19 'Welcome home, my dear,' said his wife.
20 'Eat up your nice rice pudding,' she urged. 'You'll never grow big and strong if you don't eat properly.'
21 She said, 'I'll give you £500 to keep your mouth shut.'
22 'Let's wait here till the rain stops,' she said.
23 'Curse this zip-fastener! It's stuck again,' she exclaimed.
24 'If the boys do anything clever you call them your sons,' said Mrs Smith complainingly, 'and if they do anything stupid you call them mine.'
25 'Do you know that the shoes you are wearing aren't a pair?' I said.
'Yes, but I was in a hurry this morning and these were the only ones I could find,' he said.
26 'What about going for a swim?' he said. 'It's quite fine now.'
27 'Ugh! There's a slug in my lettuce. Waiter!' he cried.

28 'Naughty boy!' said his mother, 'you've been fighting again.'
'But I didn't start it, mother,' said the boy protestingly. 'He hit me first.'

91 Indirect speech to direct speech

B PEG 292–307

Put the following into direct speech with the appropriate punctuation.

1 She asked if he'd like to go to the concert and I said that I was sure he would.
2 She told me to look where I was going as the road was full of holes and very badly lit.
3 They said that while they were bathing they saw someone examining their clothes.
4 I asked if she had looked everywhere and she said that she had.
5 He suggested giving her a bottle of wine.
6 He said that the new carpet had arrived and asked where he was to put it.
7 He said that two days previously an enormous load of firewood had been dumped at his front gate and that since then he hadn't been able to get his car out.
8 They offered me some more wine and I accepted.
9 He said that if I found the front door locked I was to go round to the back.
10 She asked the burglars who they were and who had let them in. They told her to sit down and keep quiet unless she wanted to get hurt.
11 He asked what the weather had been like during my holidays and I said that it had been awful.
12 He suggested going down to the harbour and seeing if they could hire a boat.
13 He said that if I didn't like escalators I could go up the emergency staircase. I thanked him and said that I would do that.
14 He suggested that Tom and I should go ahead and get the tickets.
15 He said that he thought my electric iron was unsafe and advised me to have it seen to.
16 He said that if war broke out he would have to leave the country at once.
17 I asked him if he had enjoyed house-hunting and he said that he hadn't.

18 She said that she was surprised to see that the grandfather clock had stopped and asked if anyone had been fiddling with it.
19 She said that she had tried to ring up her mother several times on the previous day but had not succeeded in getting through.
20 I asked her if she'd like to borrow the book but she thanked me and said that she had already read it and hadn't liked it very much.
21 He wanted to know if I was going to the dance and suggested that we should make up a party and go together.
22 I told her to stop making a fuss about nothing and said that she was lucky to have got a seat at all.
23 The clerk in the booking office inquired if I wanted a single or return ticket. I asked if a return was any cheaper. He said it made no difference.
24 My employer hoped I would not be offended if he told me that, in his opinion, I would do better in some other kind of job.
25 The A.A. man told the woman that if her wheels had gone a couple of inches nearer the edge, the car would have plunged into the ravine.
26 He said I mustn't mind if the first one wasn't any good.
27 He asked the crowd if they thought that he was a liar and the crowd shouted that they did.
28 I stopped a man in the street and asked him to help me with my car. The man asked if it would take long, explaining that he was on his way to catch a train.

92 Passive voice: active to passive

C PEG 289–91

Put the following into the passive voice. The agent should not be mentioned except in numbers 11 and 28.

1 You should open the wine about three hours before you use it.
2 Previous climbers had cut steps in the ice and fixed a rope.
3 Somebody had cleaned my shoes and brushed my suit.
4 We use this room only on special occasions.
5 You must not hammer nails into the walls without permission.
6 In some districts farmers use pigs to find truffles.
7 Someone switched on a light and opened the door.
8 Somebody had slashed the picture with a knife.
9 They are pulling down the old theatre.
10 Why didn't they mend the roof before it fell in?

11 The mob broke all the shop windows in recent riots.
12 The librarian said that they were starting a new system because people were not returning books.
13 The police asked each of us about his movements on the night of the crime.
14 Someone will serve refreshments.
15 People must not leave bicycles in the hall.
16 Members may keep books for three weeks. After that they must return them.
17 The burglars had cut an enormous hole in the steel door.
18 I've bought a harp. They are delivering it this afternoon. (*Do not change the first sentence*)
19 Someone has already told him to report for duty at six.
20 They rang the church bells as a flood warning.
21 No one can do anything unless someone gives us more information.
22 People are spending far more money on food now than they spent ten years ago.
23 The organizers will exhibit the paintings till the end of the month.
24 They will say nothing more about the matter if someone returns the stolen gun.
25 It is high time someone told him to stop behaving like a child.
26 A thief stole my dog and brought him back only when I offered £20 reward for him.
27 The judge gave him two weeks in which to pay the fine.
28 They make these artificial flowers of silk.

93 Passive voice: active to passive

C PEG 289–91

Put the following into the passive, mentioning the agent where necessary.

Where there is an indirect and a direct object, make the indirect object the subject of the passive verb.

e.g. They gave her a clock.
She was given a clock.

1 They feed the seals at the zoo twice a day.
2 Who wrote it?
3 Compare clothes which we have washed with clothes which any other laundry has washed.

4 He expected us to offer him the job.
5 They showed her the easiest way to do it.
6 Lightning struck the old oak.
7 Titian couldn't have painted it as people didn't wear that style of dress till after his death.
8 A jellyfish stung her.
9 The author has written a special edition for children.
10 Judges used to carry sweet herbs as a protection against jail-fever.
11 What did he write it with?
He wrote it with a matchstick dipped in blood.
12 An uneasy silence succeeded the shot.
13 Did the idea interest you?
14 The lawyer gave him the details of his uncle's will.
15 Beavers make these dams.
16 They used to start these engines by hand. Now they start them by electricity.
17 Most people opposed this.
18 Students are doing a lot of the work.
19 The Prime Minister was to have opened the dry dock.
20 They are to court-martial him.
21 The closure of the workshops will make a lot of men redundant.
22 Anyone with the smallest intelligence could understand these instructions.
23 We will not admit children under sixteen.
24 Boys of sixteen to eighteen are to man this training ship.
25 A rainstorm flooded the gypsies' camp.
26 The howling of wolves kept him awake all night.
27 They think that a scientist should teach science but that any idiot can teach history.
28 Children couldn't have done all this damage.

94 Active to passive with verb + preposition/adverb combinations

B PEG 290

In this exercise most of the sentences contain a verb + preposition/ adverb combination. The preposition or adverb must be retained when the combination is put into the passive.
In most of the sentences it is not necessary to mention the agent.

1 The government has called out troops.
2 Fog held up the trains. (*agent required*)
3 You are to leave this here. Someone will call for it later on.
4 We called in the police.
5 They didn't look after the children properly.
6 They are flying in reinforcements.
7 Then they called up men of 28.
8 Everyone looked up to him. (*agent required*)
9 All the ministers will see him off at the airport. (*agent required*)
10 He hasn't slept in his bed.
11 We can build on more rooms.
12 They threw him out.
13 They will have to adopt a different attitude.
14 He's a dangerous maniac. They ought to lock him up.
15 Her story didn't take them in. (*agent required*)
16 Burglars broke into the house.
17 The manufacturers are giving away small plastic toys with each packet of cereal.
18 They took down the notice.
19 They frown on smoking here.
20 After the government had spent a million pounds on the scheme they decided that it was impracticable and gave it up. (*Make only the first and last verbs passive*)
21 When I returned I found that they had towed my car away. I asked why they had done this and they told me that it was because I had parked it under a No-Parking sign. (*four passives*)
22 People must hand in their weapons.
23 The crowd shouted him down.
24 People often take him for his brother.
25 No one has taken out the cork.
26 The film company were to have used the pool for aquatic displays, but now they have changed their minds about it and are filling it in. (*Make the first and last verbs passive*)

27 This college is already full. We are turning away students the whole time.
28 You will have to pull down this skyscraper as you have not complied with the town planning regulations.

95 Active to passive with changes of construction

A PEG 291

Some of the following sentences when put into the passive require, or can have, a change of construction.

1 a **think, know, consider, believe, acknowledge, understand, find, say, claim, report,** when used in the passive are often followed by the infinitive.

e.g. *People say that he is a spy:* *It is said that he is a spy.*
or: *He is said* to be *a spy.*
People say that he was a spy: *It is said that he was a spy.*
or: *He is said* to have been *a spy.*

There is normally no difference in meaning between the two forms and the infinitive construction, being neater, is often preferred.

b **suppose** in the passive can similarly be followed by either of these constructions, but there is a difference in meaning here, because the present infinitive used after passive tenses of **suppose** usually conveys a sense of duty.

e.g. *It is supposed that you know:* *People believe that you know.*
but: *You are supposed to know:* *It is your duty to know.*

The perfect infinitive, however, does not necessarily convey this sense of duty.

i.e. *He is supposed to have written it* normally means: People believe that he wrote it.

It is supposed that he wrote is much less usual and conveys a faint hint of doubt.

2 Note that an infinitive placed after a passive verb is normally a full infinitive, i.e. an infinitive with **to**.

Therefore: *He made me work* becomes: *I was made to work*.
and: *We saw them enter* becomes: *They were seen to enter*.

3 Sentences of the type: *I got the garage to mend the puncture* are most neatly expressed in the passive by the **have** + object + past participle construction (see PEG 118).

e.g. *I had the puncture mended.*

Put the following sentences into the passive, using an infinitive construction where possible.

1 We added up the money and found that it was correct.
2 They claim that this engine is twice as powerful as the previous one.
3 Someone seems to have made a terrible mistake.
4 It is your duty to make tea at eleven o'clock. (*use* **suppose**)
5 People know that he is armed.
6 Someone saw him pick up the gun.
7 We know that you were in town on the night of the crime.
8 We believe that he has special knowledge which may be useful to the police. (*one passive*)
9 You needn't have done this.
10 It's a little too loose; you had better ask your tailor to take it in. (*one passive*)
11 He likes people to call him 'sir'.
12 Don't touch this switch.
13 You will have to get someone to see to it.
14 It is impossible to do this. (*use* **can't**)
15 Someone is following us.
16 They used to make little boys climb the chimneys to clean them. (*one passive*)
17 You have to see it to believe it. (*two passives*)
18 You order me about and I am tired of it. (I am tired of . . .)
19 He doesn't like people laughing at him.
20 You don't need to wind this watch.
21 They shouldn't have told him.
22 They say that the rocket travelled six thousand miles and landed in the target area.
23 People believe that he was killed by tribesmen.
24 They are to send letters to the leaders of charitable organizations.
25 We consider that she was the best singer that Australia has ever produced. (*one passive*)
26 We don't allow smoking.
27 We know that the expedition reached the South Pole in May.
28 Before they invented printing people had to write everything by hand.

96 Passive to active

B PEG 289–91

Turn the following sentences into the active voice. Where no agent is mentioned one must be supplied.

e.g. School notice: This door must be kept shut.
Students must keep this door shut.

1 Why don't you have your eyes tested? (*see note 3 opposite*)
2 This speed limit is to be introduced gradually.
3 The runways are being lengthened at all the main airports.
4 It is now 6 a.m. and at most of the hospitals in the country patients are being wakened with cups of tea.
5 Byron is said to have lived on vinegar and potatoes.
6 Any sturgeon that are caught by British ships must be offered to the Queen.
7 This signpost has been tampered with.
8 The owners went away last March and since then their houseboat has been used continuously by squatters. (*use a continuous tense and omit* continuously)
9 The damaged ship was being towed into harbour when the towline broke.
10 Have a lift put in and then you won't have to climb up all these stairs.
11 Last year a profit of two million pounds was made in the first six months but this was cancelled by a loss of seventeen million pounds which was made in the second six months.
12 Evening dress will be worn.
13 The ship was put into quarantine and passengers and crew were forbidden to land.
14 Someone will have to be found to take her place.
15 He was made to walk along a chalked line and repeat complicated tongue-twisters.
16 This rumour must have been started by our opponents.
17 My paintings are to be exhibited for the first time by the New Arts Gallery.
18 This scientific theory has now been proved to be false.
19 The car which was blown over the cliff yesterday is to be salvaged today.
20 The house where the dead man was found is being guarded by the police to prevent it from being entered and the evidence interfered with.

